MUSIC AND LYRICS
BY
COLE PORTER

A Treasury of Cole Porter

with an Introduction by Robert Kimball

CHAPPELL & CO., INC.
NEW YORK

RANDOM HOUSE
NEW YORK

PHOTO CREDITS:

P. 2, 5, 6, 7, 8, 9, 158: Various Cole Porter Collections
P. 4: Original pencil drawing by Lorelle Raboni
P. 15, 150: MUSEUM OF THE CITY OF NEW YORK (Theatre and Music Collection)
P. 28, 120, 278: CULVER PICTURES, INC.
P. 33, 37, 71, 111, 178: VAN DAMN PHOTOS, Theatre Collection, The New York Public Library; Astor, Lenox and Tilden Foundations
P. 96, 169: THEATRE COLLECTION, The New York Public Library; Astor, Lenox and Tilden Foundations
P. 266: Courtesy of Gretchen Wyler
P. 288: Camera Portrait by Phyfe

For all works contained herein:
International Copyright Secured ALL RIGHTS RESERVED Printed in the U.S.A.
Unauthorized copying, arranging, adapting, recording or public performance is an infringement of copyright.
Infringers are liable under the law.

A special debt of gratitude is expressed to Robert Kimball for his valued assistance in the preparation of this book and to Irving Brown and Mary Ellen Stamford of Warner Bros. Music for their co-operation and help.

ISBN 394-70794-X
Library of Congress Catalog Card Number 72-3980

Book Designed and Edited by LEE SNIDER

CONTENTS

COLE PORTER

by ROBERT KIMBALL

This book is a tribute to Cole Porter, one of America's foremost song writers. A courageous man and a great artist, Cole Porter wrote glorious music and sophisticated lyrics that splendidly evoke the times in which he lived yet have endured to bring pleasure to millions and to become a significant part of our cultural heritage. Witty, urbane, ebullient, and poignant, the best Porter songs are crafted with skill, beauty and intensity of expression that bear the subtle and unique qualities of artistic genius.

Here is the most comprehensive collection of Cole Porter songs ever published. Here, too, are the complete lyrics of many songs presented with their music for the first time in the form that most closely approximates Cole Porter's original intentions.

Born in Peru, Indiana on June 9, 1891, Cole Porter was the son of Kate Cole and Samuel Fenwick Porter. He received his formal education at Worcester Academy (1905-09), Yale College (1909-13), Harvard Law and Music Schools (1913-16), and the Schola Cantorum in Paris (1920-21). His musical education, one of the most extensive ever received by an American theatre composer, began under his mother's tutelage with the study of piano and violin. Cole's earliest attempts at composition produced such precocious, albeit pedestrian, concoctions as the *Song of the Birds* (1900) and *The Bob-O-Link Waltz* (1902). His appetite for lyric writing was whetted by his father's avid interest in classic languages and nineteenth century romantic poetry, interests that were further developed in prep school and college.

John Wilson, Noel Coward, and Cole (Venice)

It was at Yale that he first found his niche as a song writer, creating the famous football songs *Bull Dog* and *Bingo Eli Yale*. His Yale Glee Club specialties (displaying a burgeoning kinship for the lofty heights of the Keith vaudeville circuit) and the musical comedy scores he wrote for his fraternity Delta Kappa Epsilon's initiation plays and the Yale Dramatic Association have been fondly recalled by his contemporaries for their suave, audacious lyrics and captivating music that already forecast the attributes of Cole's later distinction.

Although his Yale triumphs had earmarked him for almost certain success in the theatre, his Broadway debut as the composer and co-lyricist of the comic opera *SEE AMERICA FIRST* in March, 1916 was a fiasco that lasted for only fifteen performances. (Porter had vainly sought to be the American "Gilbert & Sullivan.")

Linda and Cole on board the Chonsu

In June, 1917 he sailed for Europe to work with the Duryea Relief Organization but within a few months enlisted in the French Foreign Legion. Later in the War he was attached to the American Embassy in Paris, where on January 30, 1918, at a wedding breakfast in the Ritz Hotel for Ethel Harriman and Henry Russell, he met the exquisite Linda Lee Thomas. Linda, an elegant divorcée whom Bernard Berenson succinctly described as "a great beauty with great brains" and Cole fell in love and were married in Paris in December, 1919.

Cole Porter on the Lido in Venice (1920's)

Venice: Cole with friends. Note Fanny Brice (seated on left) and Elsa Maxwell (seated, 2nd from left)

For a substantial portion of the 1920's Cole and Linda Porter made Europe their home, especially Paris and Venice. They travelled widely and lived and entertained on a grand scale. Linda widened Cole's artistic horizons by introducing him to many outstanding cultural figures as well as leading members of international café society.

One has an almost indelible image of Cole Porter absorbed in his work in the midst of treasure hunts, beach parties, fashionable outings and costume balls. Yet this fabulous, almost unreal world, which would seem on first blush to have a stifling effect on the development of his talent, actually sharpened his satiric gifts, enriched the quality of his art, and inspired some of his most original works.

Linda and Cole with Papuan chieftain, New Guinea, March, 1935

Yet the 1920's were filled with immense professional frustration for Cole as he was thought by many to be little more than a playboy-expatriate and succeeded in placing only a few songs in stage revues both in London and New York. Nevertheless, buoyed by the constant encouragement of Linda, he continued to work. It is no secret that the songs that seem to us to have been "tossed off" with the most casual effort were in fact the product of a lifelong dedication to his profession and nights and days of the most intense labor.

He worked away from the piano, writing the words and music almost simultaneously. First he created the opening and finish of a song, then proceeded from both beginning and ending toward the middle. The results often produced songs with a special artistic unity, fresh and unhackneyed, and free of many of the cliches of the vast preponderance of the songs of that age. Then, too, Porter was aloof from the mainstream of American life. Living in "exile" in Europe, he maintained some perspective on America's headlong pursuit of material utopia.

Finally, Porter's creative doldrums — the years of professional frustration after the failure of *SEE AMERICA FIRST* — ended when Monty Wooley asked him to submit songs for a Yale Dramat Christmas show in 1925. A visit to Venice by Fanny Brice in 1927 inspired some additional songs that were sung by Miss Brice at New York's Palace Theatre. Other songs were composed for friends and were performed at private parties. One song, *I'm In Love Again,* became a favorite of bandleaders after they heard it at Bricktop's in Paris and soon Paul Whiteman's recording made it a major success. But the most memorable assisttance came from Irving Berlin, Porter's closest friend among theatre composers and a great admirer of Porter's work. He later wrote Cole that "Anything I can do, you can do better," while Porter thought Berlin to be America's best songwriter. Berlin suggested to Ray Goetz, his brother-in-law by a first marriage, that he persuade Cole to write some American songs with a French flavor for Goetz' new show *PARIS.* The show was to premiere at Berlin's Music Box Theatre in 1928 with Mrs. Goetz, the international favorite Irene Bordoni, in a starring role. The rest is theatrical history, as *Let's Do It* was a smash hit and from then on Porter's reputation was firmly established in the front ranks of the theatre.

At a recording session

The Porters attend an opening

Unlike the careers of the Gershwins, Rodgers and Hart, Vincent Youmans, DeSylva Brown and Henderson, and countless others, Cole's was no meteoric rise. He did not, as many of them did, come from the ranks of Tin Pan Alley via the traditional route of song plugger, rehearsal pianist, and vaudeville accompanist. His family wealth, while obviating the necessity of seeking this kind of employment, may have been a subtle barrier to his achievement.

With success Porter, in his own words, expanded like "a night-blooming flower." Shows such as *WAKE UP AND DREAM* (1929), *FIFTY MILLION FRENCHMEN* (1929), *THE NEW YORKERS* (1930), *GAY DIVORCE* (1932), *ANYTHING GOES* (1934) *JUBILEE* (1935), *RED HOT AND BLUE* (1936), *DuBARRY WAS A LADY* (1939), and countless others boasted numerous hit songs that buoyed the nation's spirits during the Depression. But it is not true that his most famous songs, *Night And Day* and *Begin The Beguine,* were failures when they were introduced. Nor is it true, as some allege, that Porter's creativity "dried up" after the tragic riding accident he suffered in October, 1937 which required over thirty operations and kept him in constant pain for the remainder of his life. A careful examination of the songs in this book reveals ample evidence of the continuing strength of his creativity.

Cole Porter died on October 15, 1964 and now, almost eight years after his death, we are in the midst of what many people are calling a "Porter revival." Actually, while Porter's popularity has never waned, it is true that in the past few years his work has become more popular and more admired today than ever before. Hopefully, this volume will refresh the recollections of those who know and love his work and introduce thousands of others to the music and lyrics of a creator who shared his gifts with all of us, who challenged our intelligence, chronicled our foibles, and made us laugh and cry as he touched our hearts.

Mr. Kimball is the author of COLE, published by Holt, Rinehart & Winston.

LET'S DO IT
LET'S FALL IN LOVE

"Paris"

Words and Music by
COLE PORTER

Moderato

Piano

mp cresc. mf

Gm F7
Semplice (not fast) Bb F7

When the lit - tle Blue-bird, Who has nev - er said a word, Starts to

poco rit p a tempo.

Bb Bb+ Gm Bb+ Bb F+ Gm F7

sing:"Spring, spring," When the lit - tle Blue - bell, In the

mf p

Copyright © 1928 by Harms, Inc.
Copyright Renewed
All rights reserved
Reprinted by permission of WARNER BROS. MUSIC

B♭ F7 B♭ B♭+ Gm B♭+ B♭ B♭+
bot - tom of the dell, Starts to ring: "Ding, ding," When the
mf
Cm7 Cm7(♭5) B♭ C7 F7
lit - tle blue clerk, In the mid - dle of his work, Starts a
B♭ Bdim. F7 F+ B♭ B♭7
p
tune to the moon up a - bove, — It is na - ture, that's all, Simp - ly
p
E♭ E♭m B♭ F+
mf
tell - ing us to fall in love. And that's why
8va
mf f mf

Refrain
p-mf gracefully
Gm Bb F7 Bb
1 Birds do it, Bees do it, E-ven ed-u-cat-ed
2 Spon-ges, they say, do it, Oy-sters, down in Oy-ster
p-mf
Cm Cm7(b5) Gm Bb F7 Bb Ebm
fleas do it, Let's do it, Let's fall in love.
Bay, do it, Let's do it, Let's fall in love.
Bb F+ Gm Bb F7
mf p
In Spain, the best up-per sets do it,
Cold Cape Cod clams, 'gainst their wish, do it,
mf p

B♭
Cm
Cm7(♭5)
Gm
B♭
Lith - u - an - i - ans and Letts do it,
Let's do it,
Ev - en laz - y Jel - ly - fish do it,
Let's do it,
F7
B♭
Cm7
B♭
mf
Gm
Let's fall in love.
The Dutch in old Am - ster -
Let's fall in love.
E - lect - ric eels, I might
mf
Cm7
B♭
B♭7
mp
E♭
dam do it,
Not to men - tion the Finns
Folks in Si -
add, do it,
Though it shocks 'em I know.
Why ask if
mp

A♭7 D♭ B♭m7 F7 F+ Gm B♭
mf
p
- am do it, — Think of Si - am - ese twins. Some Ar - gen - tines, with - out —
shad do it, — Wait - er, bring me shad - roe. In shal - low shoals, Eng - lish —
mf
p
F7 Gm E♭7
cresc.
means, do it, — Peo - ple say, in Bos - ton, ev - en beans do it, —
soles do it, — Gold - fish, in the pri - va - cy of bowls, do it, —
cresc.
B♭ Gm Cm7(♭5) F7 B♭ E♭m B♭ F+ B♭
un poco allarg.
a tempo
1.
2.
mf
Let's do it, — let's fall in — love.
2. Ro - man - tic
Let's do it, — let's fall in — love.
mf un poco allarg.
a tempo
mf
sf
Ped.

LET'S DO IT

REFRAIN 2

The nightingales, in the dark, do it,
Larks, k-razy for a lark, do it,
Let's do it, let's fall in love.
Canaries, caged in the house, do it,
When they're out of season, grouse do it,
Let's do it, let's fall in love.
The most sedate barnyard fowls do it,
When a chantacleer cries,
High-browed old owls do it,
They're supposed to be wise,
Penguins in flocks, on the rocks, do it,
Even little cuckoos in their clocks, do it,
Let's do it, let's fall in love.

REFRAIN 4

The dragon flies, in the reeds, do it,
Sentimental centipedes do it,
Let's do it, let's fall in love.
Mosquitos, heaven forbid, do it,
So does ev'ry katydid, do it,
Let's do it, let's fall in love.
The most refined lady-bugs do it,
When a gentleman calls,
Moths in your rugs, do it,
What's the use of moth-balls?
Locusts in trees do it, bees do it,
Even highly educated fleas do it,
Let's do it, let's fall in love.

REFRAIN 5

The chimpanzees in the zoos do it,
Some courageous kangaroos do it,
Let's do it, let's fall in love.
I'm sure giraffes, on the sly, do it,
Heavy hippopotami do it,
Let's do it, let's fall in love.
Old sloths who hang down from twigs do it,
Though the effort is great,
Sweet guinea-pigs do it,
Buy a couple and wait.
The world admits bears in pits do it,
Even pekineses in the Ritz, do it,
Let's do it, let's fall in love.

Copyright © 1928 by Harms, Inc.
Copyright Renewed

Irene Bordoni, Arthur Margetson in PARIS (1928)

WHAT IS THIS THING CALLED LOVE?

"Wake Up And Dream"

Words and Music by
COLE PORTER

Copyright © 1929 by Harms, Inc.
Copyright Renewed
All rights reserved
Reprinted by permission of WARNER BROS. MUSIC

Fm
F♯dim.
G
A7
quick-ened my hum-drum heart.
Love flew in through my win-dow,
Cm
D7
G
G7
C7
F7
Dm7(♭5)
I was so hap-py then.
But af-ter love had stayed a lit-tle while,
G-
C
Dm7
G7
C
Love flew out a-gain.

REFRAIN
mp-mf Slow (in the manner of a "Blues")
C7
Fm
What is this thing called love? This
mp-mf
marked (but not too loud)
G7
G+
C
Cmaj.
C
C7
funny thing called love? Just who can solve
(simile)
C♯dim.
C7°
Fm
G7
its mys - ter - y? Why should it make
G+
C
C7
Fm
C
Cm
F7
a fool of me? I saw you there

B♭
A♭
A♭+
one won-der-ful day.
You took my heart
Fm
G
Am7
G7
Guitar tacet
C
and threw it a - way
That's why I ask the Lawd
C♯dim.
C7°
Fm
G7
G+
in Heav-en a - bove,
What is this thing called
1.
C
Fm
C
C7
2.
C
Fm
C
love?
What
love?
mf
rall. e dim.
Ped.

LOVE FOR SALE

"The New Yorkers"

Words and Music by
COLE PORTER

Copyright © 1930 by Harms, Inc.
Copyright Renewed
All rights reserved
Reprinted by permission of WARNER BROS. MUSIC

A♭ A♭7 F F7 B♭
smirk, I go to work.
REFRAIN (with swinging rhythm and not fast)
p-mf
E♭ B♭m E♭
Love for sale, Ap-pe-tiz-ing young love for
B♭m E♭ A♭7 D♭ E♭m
sale. Love that's fresh and still un-spoiled, Love that's on-ly slight-ly soiled,
B♭m F7+5 B♭m E♭ B♭
Love for sale. Who will buy?
p

E♭ B♭ E♭
Who would like to sam-ple my sup-ply? Who's pre-pared to
A♭7 D♭ E♭m B♭m F7 B♭m
pay the price For a trip to par-a-dise? Love for sale.
B♭m7 E♭m7 A♭7 D♭
mp espress.
Let the po-ets pipe of love In their child-ish way,
mp espress.
E♭m7 A♭7 D♭ B♭m7 B♭7
I know ev-'ry type of love Bet-ter far than, they. If you want the
E♭m G♭ E♭m Edim. C7
mf espress.
thrill of love, I've been thru the mill of love; Old love, new love,
mf espress.

B7 rall. Bdim. più rit. Bb7(-5) Eb f a tempo Bbm
Ev-'ry love but true love. Love for sale,
rall.
più rit.
f a tempo
Eb Bb Eb
Ap-pe-tiz-ing young love for sale. If you want to
Ab7 Db molto cresc. Ebm F+ ff broadly
buy my wares, Fol-low me and climb the stairs, Love for
molto cresc.
ff broadly
Bbm dimin. Bbm7 Bbm6 p Eb7 F+
sale. Love for
dimin.
p
E dim. p dim. e morendo Ebm6 1. Bb 2. Bb
sale. sale.
pp
p dim. e morendo

NIGHT AND DAY

"Gay Divorce"

Words and Music by
COLE PORTER

Copyright © 1932 by Harms, Inc.
Copyright Renewed
All rights reserved
Reprinted by permission of WARNER BROS. MUSIC

D Dm B° C Cm G B♭m6 C G7 C
through; So a voice with-in me keeps re-peat-ing, you, you, you.
Refrain
C6 Cm G7 G+ C
p-mf
Night and day you are the one, On-ly you-
p-mf
Cm G7 G+ C Am
be-neath the moon and un-der the sun. Wheth-er near to me or
A♭ Em7 D7 F♯m D7 Bm F Fm F
far, It's no mat-ter, dar-ling, where you are I think of you
R. H.

G7 C Cm G7 G+
night and day. Day and night Why is it
C Cm G7 G+ C
so, That this long - ing for you fol-lows wher-ev-er I go?
C Am A♭ Em7 D7 F#m D7 Bm
In the roar-ing traf-fic's boom In the si-lence of my lone-ly room, I
R. H.
F Fm F G7 C E♭
think of you, night and day. Night and day
mf espr.

E♭ C E♭ Fm E♭
— un-der the hide of me ——— There's an Oh, such a hun-gry yearn-
Fm E♭ C Am
- ing, burn - ing in - side of me. ——— And its tor - ment won't be
A♭ Em7 D7 Dm7
through — 'Til you let me spend my life mak-ing love — to you, day and night, ———
G7 Dm7 1. C D7 G7 2. C
— night and day. — Night and day — ———
mf
mf
f
8

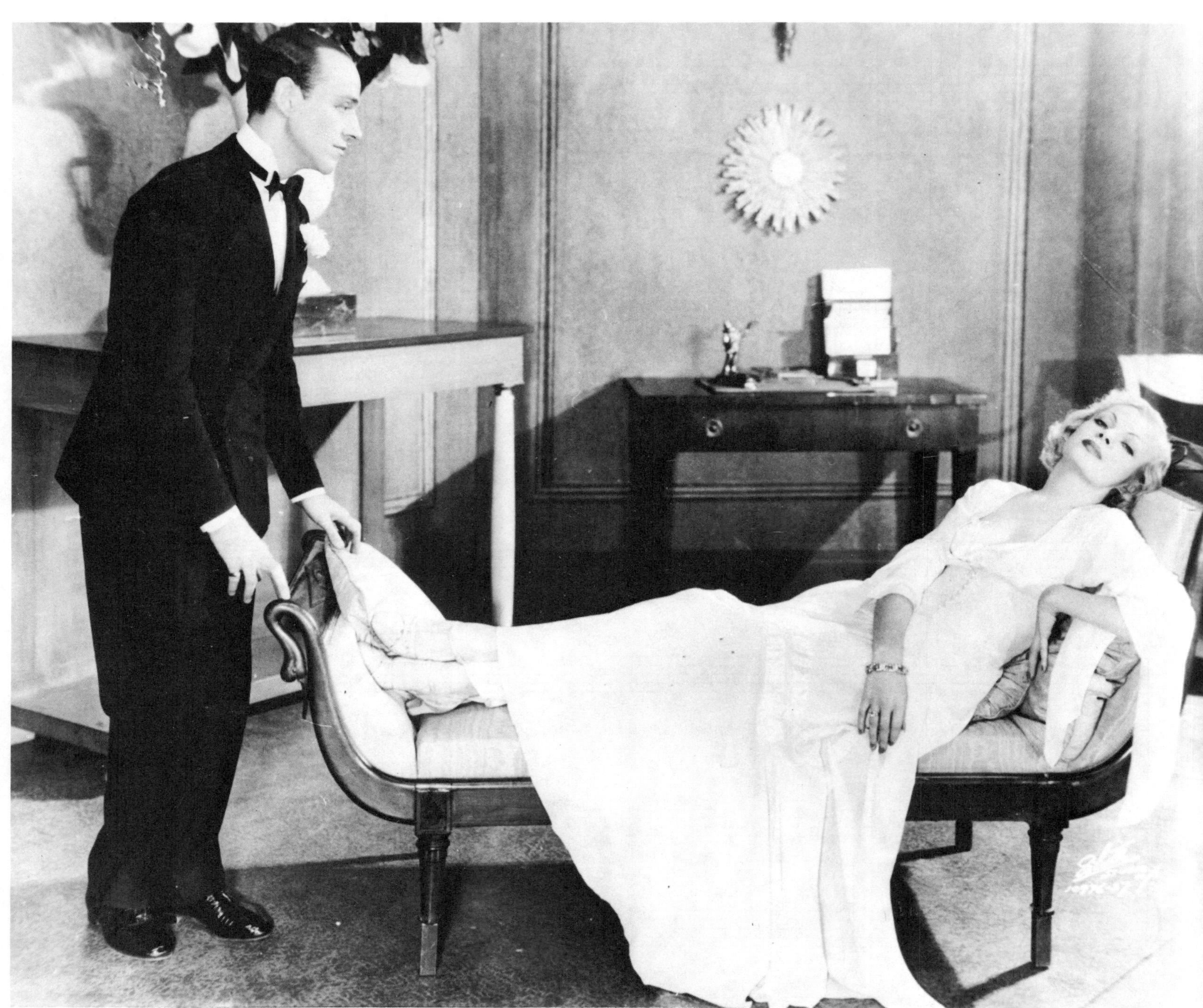

Fred Astaire and Claire Luce in a scene from THE GAY DIVORCE (1932)

I GET A KICK OUT OF YOU

"Anything Goes"

Words and Music by
COLE PORTER

Copyright © 1934 by Harms, Inc.
Copyright Renewed
All rights reserved
Reprinted by permission of WARNER BROS. MUSIC

C7
Fm
B♭7
E♭
Gm
And I sud-den-ly turn and see _ your fab-u-lous face.
REFRAIN
Fm7 Fm6 Fm7 B♭7 E♭ Gm Fm7 Fm6 Fm7
p-mf
I get no kick from cham - pagne, _____ Mere al - co -
p-mf
B♭7 E♭ Gm Fm7 B♭7 E♭
hol does - n't thrill me at all, So tell me why should it be true. _____
Gm7 Fm B♭7 E♭ Gm
_ That I get a kick _ out of you? _____

Fm7 Fm6 Fm7 B♭7 E♭ Gm Fm7 Fm6 Fm7
Some like a bop type re - frain I'm sure that
B♭7 E♭ Cm6 Gm Fm7 F7 B♭ A A♭
if I heard ev - en one riff That would bore me ter - rif - ic - 'ly
E♭ Gm Fm B♭7 E♭
too. Yet I get a kick out of you.
Gm E♭7 A♭ E♭7 D♭ A♭ D♭ A♭
mf
I get a kick ev - 'ry time I see you're
mf
Cm E♭7 Cm E♭7 Edim. C7
stand - ing there be - fore me.

Fm B♭m6 Fm B♭m6 Fm F7
p
I get a kick tho' it's clear to me You ob - vious -
p
Fm7 B♭7 Fm7 Fm6 Fm7 B♭7
ly don't a - dore me. I get no kick in a
E♭ Gm Fm7 Fm6 Fm7 B♭7 E♭
plane, Fly - ing too high with some {gal guy} in the
Gm Fm7 B♭7 C7
sky Is my i - dea of noth - ing to do. Yet
Fm7 B♭7 1. E♭ Gm 2. E♭
I get a kick out of you. you.
mf
f

YOU'RE THE TOP

VERSE 2

Your words poetic are not pathetic
On the other hand, boy, you shine
And I can feel after every line
A thrill divine
Down my spine.
Now gifted humans like Vincent Youmans
Might think that your song is bad,
But for a person who's just rehearsin'
Well I gotta say this my lad:

REFRAIN 3

You're the top!
You're a Ritz hot toddy.
You're the top!
You're a Brewster body.
You're the boats that glide on the sleepy Zuider Zee,
You're a Nathan panning,
You're a Bishop Manning,
You're broccoli.
You're a prize,
You're a night at Coney,
You're the eyes
Of Irene Bordoni.
I'm a broken doll, a fol-de-rol, a blop,
But if, Baby, I'm the bottom
You're the top!

REFRAIN 4

You're the top!
You're an Arrow collar.
You're the top!
You're a Coolidge dollar.
You're the nimble tread of the feet of Fred Astaire,
You're an O'Neill drama,
You're Whistler's mama,
You're Camembert.
You're a rose,
You're Inferno's Dante,
You're the nose
On the great Durante.
I'm just in the way, as the French would say
"De trop,"
But if, Baby, I'm the bottom
You're the top.

REFRAIN 5

You're the top!
You're a Waldorf salad.
You're the top!
You're a Berlin ballad.
You're a baby grand of a lady and a gent,
You're an old Dutch master,
You're Mrs. Astor,
You're Pepsodent.
You're romance,
You're the steppes of Russia,
You're the pants on a Roxy usher.
I'm a lazy lout that's just about to stop,
But if, Baby, I'm the bottom
You're the top.

REFRAIN 6

You're the top!
You're a dance in Bali.
You're the top!
You're a hot tamale.
You're an angel, you, simply too, too, too diveen,
You're a Botticelli,
You're Keats,
You're Shelley,
You're Ovaltine.
You're a boon,
You're the dam at Boulder,
You're the moon over Mae West's shoulder.
I'm a nominee of the G.O.P.
or GOP,
But if, Baby, I'm the bottom,
You're the top.

Ethel Merman, William Gaxton in ANYTHING GOES (1934)

REFRAIN 7

You're the top!
You're the Tower of Babel.
You're the top!
You're the Whitney Stable.
By the River Rhine,
You're a sturdy stein of beer,
You're a dress from Saks's,
You're next year's taxes,
You're stratosphere.
You're my thoist,
You're a Drumstick Lipstick,
You're da foist
In da Irish svipstick.
I'm a frightened frog
That can find no log
To hop,
But, if, Baby, I'm the bottom,
You're the top!

Copyright © 1934 by Harms, Inc.
Copyright Renewed

YOU'RE THE TOP

"Anything Goes"

Words and Music by
COLE PORTER

Copyright © 1934 by Harms, Inc.
Copyright Renewed
All rights reserved
Reprinted by permission of WARNER BROS. MUSIC

Gm Cm6 Gm F7 B♭7 (Guitar tacet) B♭+
if this dit-ty Is not so pret-ty At least it-'ll tell you how great you are.
REFRAIN
E♭ B° E♭ E° B♭7 B♭6
You're the top! You're the Col-os-se-um,
You're the top! You're Ma-hat-ma Ghan-di,
p - mf
E♭ Cm G7
You're the top! You're the Louvr' Mu-se-um,
You're the top! You're Na-po-leon bran-dy,
A♭ Fm7 B♭7 Fm7 B♭ E♭ B♭
You're a mel-o-dy From a sym-pho-ny by
You're the pur-ple light Of a sum-mer night in
Cm D Gm C9 F7 B♭9 E°
Strauss, You're a Ben-del bon-net, A Shake-speare son-net, You're Mick-y Mouse.
Spain, You're the Na-tion'l Gall'-ry, You're Gar-bo's sal-'ry, You're cel-o-phane,
mf

You're the Nile, You're the Tow'r of Pi-sa, You're the smile on the Mo-na Lis-a; I'm a worth-less check, a to-tal wreck, a flop,
You're sub-lime, You're a tur-key din-ner, You're the time of the Der-by win-ner, I'm a toy bal-loon that is fat-ed soon to pop;
But if Ba-by, I'm the bot-tom, You're the top!
top!
(Guitar tacet)

ne Knight and Charles Walters dance BEGIN THE BEGUINE in JUBILEE (1935)

JUST ONE OF THOSE THINGS

"Jubilee"

Words and Music by
COLE PORTER

Copyright © 1935 by Harms, Inc.
Copyright Renewed
All rights reserved
Reprinted by permission of WARNER BROS. MUSIC

G♯dim. F Em7(♭5) C♯dim. A7 Dm F7 B♭ G♯dim.
"Don't for-get to drop a line to me, please", As Jul-iet cried
F Cm D7 Gm sus4 Gm Dm Gm7 A7
in her Ro-meo's ear, "Ro-meo, why not face the fact, my dear?"
A7
REFRAIN
Dm A F7
p-mf
It was just one of those things, Just one
Bm7(♭5) C♯dim. F Fm Gm7 C7
of those cra-zy flings. One of those bells that now and then rings,

Dm7 F♯dim. C7 A7 Dm
Just one of those things. It was just one of those
A F7 Bm7(♮5) C♯dim. F
nights, Just one of those fab-u-lous flights, A trip to the
G♯dim. F Gm7 C7 Dm7 F♯dim. Fm7 B♭7
moon on gos-sa-mer wings, Just one of those things. If we'd
E♭ B♭7 E♭ G7
thought a bit of the end of it When we start-ed paint-ing the town,

Am7
F♯dim. 7(♮5)
Fm7
mf
Dm7(♭5) Em7
D
We'd have been a - ware That our love af - fair Was too hot not
cresc.
mf
F♭dim.
C
p
A7
Dm
A
to cool down.
So good-bye, dear, and A - men,
p
F7
B♭
Gm7
Am
D7
Here's hop - ing we meet now and then,
It was great fun, But it was
F♯dim.
Gm
C7
F
Am
Dm
F
1 Gm
A7
mf
A7
2. F
just one of those things.
It was
mf
mf

BEGIN THE BEGUINE

"Jubilee"

Words and Music by
COLE PORTER

Copyright © 1935 by Harms, Inc.
Copyright Renewed
All rights reserved
Reprinted by permission of WARNER BROS. MUSIC

C
C6
Cmaj. 7
C6
I'm with you once more under the stars And
C
G7
down by the shore an or-ches-tra's play - ing, And e-ven the palms
Dm
G7
F
Dm7
G7
G7 sus4
G7
seem to be sway - ing When they be-gin the Be-
C
Cm
F7
B♭
guine. To live it a - gain is past all en-deav - our,

B♭m E♭7 A♭maj. 7 A♭6 A♭
Ex-cept when that tune clutch-es my heart, And
cresc.
A° più espr. F♯° G A♭
mf
there we are, swear-ing to love for-ev - er, And prom-is-ing
mf più espr.
G Fm7 G G7 C
dim.
p
nev - er nev - er to part. What mo-ments di-vine,
dim.
p
C6 Cmaj. 7 C6 C C7
what rap-ture se-rene, Till clouds came a-long to dis-perse the joys we had

G7
Fm
Dm7(-5)
tast - ed,
And now when I hear peo-ple curse the chance that was wast - ed,
Fm
G7
G7(sus4)
G7
C sus D
C
I know but too well
what they mean;
So don't
C
più espr.
C6
C maj. 7
C6
mf
let them be - gin
the Be - guine,
Let the
mf più espr.
C
C6
C
G7
love that was once a - fire re-main an em - ber;
Let it

F
Dm7
Em
Am
Dm7
dim.
p
sleep like the dead de-sire I on-ly re-mem - ber
When they be-gin
dim.
p
G7
C6
C
molto espr.
C6
C
f
the Be-guine.
Oh yes, let them be - gin the Be - guine, make them
f molto espr.
Cmaj. 7
C6
C
play
Till the stars that were there be-fore re - turn a -
G7
mf
F
Dm7
Em
dim.
bove you,
Till you whis-per to me once more, "Dar-ling, I love you!"
mf
dim.

A9
Dm7
Dm7(-5)
p
And we sud-den-ly know what heav-en we're in,
G7
C
Cmaj. 7
When they be - gin the Be - guine,
Dm7/C ped.
Fm6/C ped.
G7
rit.
ten.
When they be - gin the Be-
C
a tempo
dim.
C6
Cmaj. 7
pp
guine.

I'VE GOT YOU UNDER MY SKIN

"Born To Dance"

Copyright © 1936 by Chappell & Co., Inc.
Copyright Renewed

Fm7
Bb7
Ebmaj. 7
Eb6
got you under my skin.
I
p
Fm7
Bb7
Ebmaj. 7
Eb6
tried so not to give in,
I
Abm6
Bb7
D
Ebmaj. 7
Eb6
said to my-self,"This af - fair nev- er will go so well." But
Dm7
G7
D#dim.
C
why should I try to re - sist when, dar-ling, I know so well I've
mf
marcato

A♭6
A♭m
B♭7
E♭maj. 7
E♭6
got you under my skin. I'd
Fm7
B♭7
E♭
E♭7
poco a poco cresc. ed appassionato
sac-ri-fice an-y-thing, Come what might, for the sake of hav-ing you near, In spite of a
A♭
A♭m
E♭
B♭7
molto cresc.
warn-ing voice that comes in the night And re-peats and re-peats in my ear: "Don't you
subito p
Cm
f molto espressivo
A♭
B♭7
E♭
E♭dim.
know, lit-tle fool, you nev-er can win, Use your men-

Fm7
Bb7
Eb
Bb+
Eb
mf
-tal - i - ty, Wake up to re - al - i - ty." But each
mf
Ab
cresc.
Abm
Eb
p rit.
Bbm
C7
Guitar tacet
time I do, just the thought of you makes me stop, Be-fore I be - gin, 'Cause I've
cresc.
p rit.
p dolce
Fm
a tempo
Bb7(9b)
Eb
1.
poco rit
got you under my skin. I've
a tempo
rit.
ppp a tempo
poco rit.
2. Fm7
Bb7
Eb
Bb7
Eb
poco rall.
più rall.
R.H.
morendo
ppp
8

EASY TO LOVE

"Born To Dance"

Words and Music by
COLE PORTER

Copyright © 1936 by Chappell & Co., Inc.
Copyright Renewed

B♭
F7
B♭
Gm
E7♭5
I'm sure you hate to hear ___ That I a - dore you, dear, But
D
G
A7
D
E♭7
grant me, just the same, ___ I'm not en - tire - ly to blame, For
rit.
Refrain (slowly, with much expression)
Am
Dm
Am
D7
G
A♯dim. G
Am
You'd be so eas - y to love, So eas - y to i - dol - ize, all
p a tempo
G
Gm
Am7
D7
G
C♯dim.
oth - ers a - bove, So worth the yearn-ing for, ___
mf

Am7 D7 Bm C dim. Am
So swell to keep ev-'ry home-fire burn - ing for, We'd
Dm Am D7 G A♯dim. G Am G
be so grand at the game, So care-free to - geth-er, that it does seem a
E7 Am Cm6 G A♯dim. B7
shame, That you can't see Your fu - ture with me, 'Cause you'd be
Am7 D7 1. G D7 G F dim. 2. G D7 G
oh, so eas - y to love! love!
p
mf

I'VE GOT YOU UNDER MY SKIN

BORN TO DANCE

WORDS AND MUSIC BY

COLE PORTER

STARRING

Eleanor

POWELL

AND BIG MUSICAL COMEDY CAST

A

Metro-

Goldwyn-

Mayer

PICTURE

CHAPPELL

& CO · INC ·

609 FIFTH AVE.

NEW YORK 17,

N.Y.

CHAPPELL

& CO·LTD·LONDON

MADE IN U.S.A.

PRICE

75¢

Original sheet music title page for BORN TO DANCE (1936)

GOODBYE, LITTLE DREAM, GOODBYE

"Red, Hot and Blue"

Words and Music by
COLE PORTER

Copyright © 1936 by Chappell & Co., Inc.
Copyright Renewed

F♯dim. B7 E7 A♭7 G7 G7♭5 C7(9) C7 F Dm
took it straight to my heart; My fears were right,
Gm C7 F Dm Gm A
And now we must part.
mf
Refrain
Dm
slowly with tender expression
p
F+ Dm7 Bm7(♮5) C♯dim. A7
Good - bye, lit - tle dream, good - bye, You
dolce ed espressivo
p marcato
Dm F+ Dm7 Bm7(♮5) C7
made my ro - mance sub - lime, now it's time to fly. For the
marcato

F
mp più espr. e crescendo
A7
Dm
stars have fled_ from the Heav - ens,___ The moon's des - ert - ed the
mp più espr. e crescendo
Am
p
B♭
A
D7
G
hill And the sul - try breeze_ that sang in the trees,_ is
p
B♭7
A
p
A7
Dm
sud - den - ly strange - ly still. It's done,___
p
F+
Dm7
Bm7(♮5)
C♯dim.
A7
D7
crescendo
_ lit-_tle dream, it's done,___ So bid me a fond fare - well._
crescendo

Gm
D7
Gm
mp
— We both had our fun, —
Was it
f
mp
B♭
C7
F
rall.
F
Ro - me - o — or Ju - liet, Who said when a - bout to
rall.
Gm7(♭5)
p a tempo
F
A7(♭5)
D7
D♭7
C7
die, "Love is not all peach-es and cream, — Lit-tle dream, good - bye." —
8
p a tempo
1
F
Gm
A7
2.
F
Fmaj. 7
Good -
8va
pp
8

DOWN IN THE DEPTHS
ON THE NINETIETH FLOOR

"Red, Hot and Blue"

Words and Music by
COLE PORTER

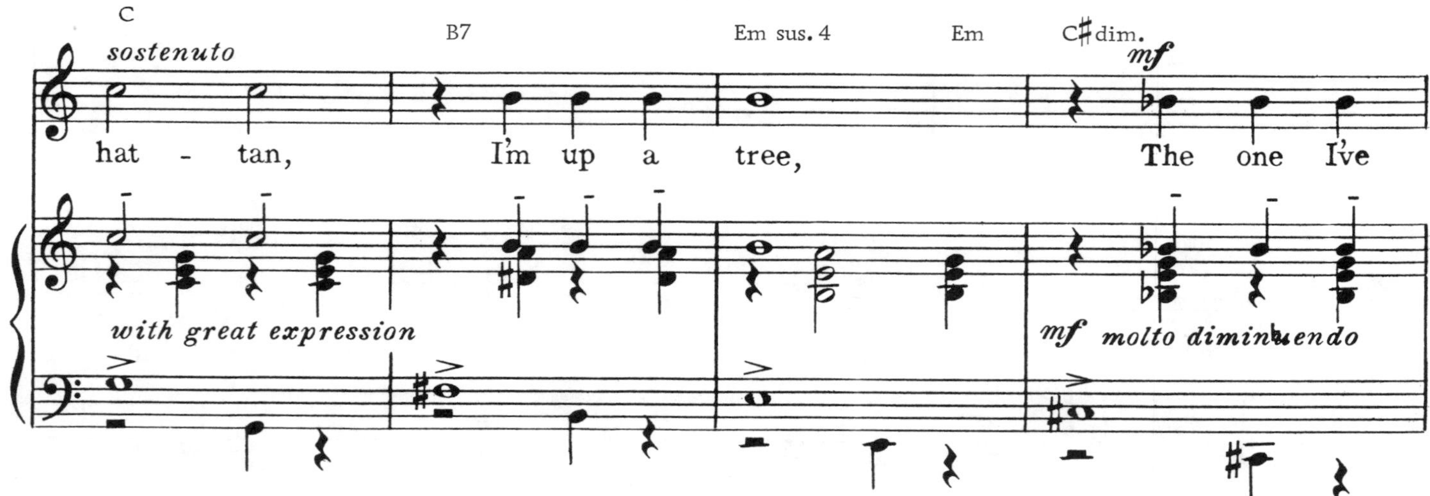

Copyright © 1936 by Chappell & Co., Inc.
Copyright Renewed

C7
B7
Em sus. 4
dim.
Em
C♯dim
p
hat - tan, I'm awf-'lly nice, Nice peo - ple
dim.
p
Gm
D
A7
mf
D
F♯m7(5♮)
p
dine with me and e - ven twice. Yet, the
mf
p
F♯7
B7
E7
B♭+
Guitar tacet
on - ly one in the world I'm mad a - bout Talks of
D
mf
Em7(♭5)
Dsus. 4
ten.
D
some-bod-y else,- And walks out.
ten.
mf
freely

D
D
Refrain (strict slow fox-trot tempo)
p-mf
With a mil - lion Ne - on rain - bows burn - ing be -
p-mf
A7
D
D
low me, And a mil - lion blaz - ing tax - is rais-ing a
Em7
Em7
G7
roar, Here I sit a - bove the town, In my
Em7(♭5)
A7
pet pail - let - ted gown, Down in the depths on the

A7 G A7 D B♭+ Bm B♭+ D
nine - tieth floor, While the
While the
A7 D
crowds in all the nightclubs punish the parquet,
crowds at El Marocco punish the parquet,
D Em7
And the bars are packed with couples calling for more,
And at Twenty One the couples clamor for more,
Em7 G7 Em7(♭5)
I'm deserted and depressed In my regal eagle
mp

A7
G A7
D
A7
cresc.
nest, Down in the depths, — on the nine - ti-eth floor,
cresc.
E♯dim.
D7 Am
mf
C
D7
C
D7
C
D
When the on - ly one you want - ed wants an - oth - er,
mf
G♯dim.
D
B7(9)
F
B7(9)
What's the use of swank and cash in the bank ga -
Fm sus. 4
Em
D♯ dim.
Em
C♯7
F♯7
lore? Why ev - en the jan - i - tor's wife Has a
Why ev - en the jan - i - tor's wife Has some

B7
E7
Em7(♭5)
A7
per-fect-ly good love-life, And here am I,
facing to-
sen-ti-ment in here life, And here am I,
D
Dm7
Am
B7
molto
mor - row,
A-lone with my sor row,
Down in the
molto
Em7
crescendo
G
Dsus. 4
1. D
G A7
mf
D
depths, on the nine - ti-eth floor.
With a
f
crescendo
mf
2. D
C
D C
D
floor.
f marcato
mf
p

IT'S DE-LOVELY

"Red, Hot and Blue"

Words and Music by
COLE PORTER

Copyright © 1936 by Chappell & Co., Inc.
Copyright Renewed

F
F♯dim.
C7
SHE:
F
F7
Gm
verse. This verse I've start - ed seems to me — the
C7
F
Dm7
G7
Tin Pan-ti - thes-is of mel - o - dy, — So to spare you all the
Gm6
A7
Dm
F
Bdim.
G7
C
pain. I'll skip the darn thing and sing the re - frain.
HE:
B♭
A♭
C7
spoken
SHE:
mi mi mi mi re re re re, Do sol mi do la si. Take it a - way!

Refrain Very rhythmically
C7+
F
F+
F
The night is young, The skies are clear And if you want to go
p-mf
walk - ing, dear, It's de - light - ful, it's de - li - cious, it's de -
F♯dim.
C7
D7
Gm
love - ly. I un - der - stand the
sf
p
E♭maj. 7
Em7 (♭5)
Gm
E♭
Em7(♭5)
Gm
reas - on why You're sent - i - ment - al, 'cause so am I, It's de -

G♯dim.
F
-light - ful, it's de - li - cious, it's de - love - ly.
G7
C7
F7
You can tell at a glance What a
mf
B♭
F7
F+
B♭
B♭m6
swell night this is for ro-mance, You can hear dear Moth - er
C7
Na-ture mur - mur-ing low. "Let your - self go." So
sf

☆ *Pronounced* "delukes".

IT'S DE-LOVELY

VERSE 2

She: Oh, charming sir, the way you sing
Would break the heart of Missus Crosby's Bing,
For the tone of your tra la la
Has that certain je ne sais quoi.
He: Oh, thank thee kindly, winsome wench,
But 'stead of falling into Berlitz French
Just warble to me, please,
This beautiful strain in plain Brooklynese.
She: Mi, mi, mi, mi,
Re, re, re, re,
Do, sol, mi, do, la, si
He: Take it away.

REFRAIN 2

Time marches on and soon it's plain
You've won my heart and I've lost my brain,
It's delightful, it's delicious, it's de-lovely.
Life seems so sweet that we decide
It's in the bag to get unified,
It's delightful, it's delicious, it's de-lovely.
See the crowd in that church,
See the proud parson plopped on his perch,
Get the sweet beat of that organ, sealing
our doom,
"Here goes the groom, boom!"
How they cheer and how they smile
As we go galloping down that aisle.
"It's divine, dear, it's diveen, dear,
It's de-wunderbar, it's de victory,
It's de vallop, it's de vinner, it's de voiks,
it's de-lovely."

REFRAIN 3

The knot is tied and so we take
A few hours off to eat wedding cake,
It's delightful, it's delicious, it's de-lovely.
It feels so fine to be a bride,
And how's the groom? Why, he's slightly fried,
It's delightful, it's delicious, it's de-lovely.
To the pop of champagne,
Off we hop in our plush little plane
Till a bright light through the darkness
cozily calls
"Niag'ra Falls."
All's well, my love, our day's complete,
And what a beautiful bridal suite,
"It's a d-reamy, it's de-rowsy,
It's de-reverie, it's de-rhapsody,
It's de-regal, it's de-royal, it's de-Ritz,
it's de-lovely."

REFRAIN 4

We settle down as man and wife
To solve the riddle called "married life,"
It's delightful, it's delicious, it's de-lovely.
We're on the crest, we have no cares,
We're just a couple of honey bears,
It's delightful, it's delicious, it's de-lovely.
All's as right as can be
Till, one night, at my window I see
An absurd bird with a bundle hung on his nose—
"Get baby clo'es."
Those eyes of yours are filled with joy
When Nurse appears and cries, "It's a boy,"
"He's appalling, he's appealing,
He's a polywog, he's a paragon,
He's a Pop-eye, he's a panic, he's a pip,
he's de-lovely."

REFRAIN 5

Our boy grows up, he's six feet, three,
He's so good looking, he looks like me,
It's delightful, it's delicious, it's de-lovely.
He's such a hit, this son of ours,
That all the dowagers send him flowers,
It's delightful, it's delicious, it's de-lovely.
So sublime is his press
That in time, L. B. Mayer, no less,
Makes a night flight to New York and tells him he should
Go Hollywood.
Good God!, today, he gets such pay
That Elaine Barrie's his fiancé,
"It's delightful, it's delicious,
"It's delectable, it's delirious,
"It's dilemma, it's delimit, it's deluxe, it's de-lovely."

Copyright © 1936 by Chappell & Co., Inc.
Copyright Renewed

Members of the cast: RED, HOT AND BLUE (1936)

RIDIN' HIGH

"Red, Hot and Blue"

Words and Music by
COLE PORTER

Copyright © 1936 by Chappell & Co., Inc.
Copyright Renewed

D♭
Now to - geth - er We can weath - er an - y - thing.
G
F
Dm7
So, please, don't sput - ter If I should mut - ter.
Refrain
Cmaj. 7
C7
Cm7(♭5)
Gm7
G7
B
mf - f
Life's great, life's grand,
Fu - ture all planned.

E7
D
E7
Am
Dm7
No more clouds in the sky,
B
C
G7
A7
C♯dim.
Dm7
G7
C
A♭7
G7
How'm I rid-in'? I'm rid-in' high.
Cmaj. 7
C7
Cm7(♭5)
C7
Gm7
G7
B
G7
mf
Some one I love,
Cmaj. 7
C7
Cm7(♭5)
C7
Gm7
G7
B
G7
E7
Mad for my love, So long

D E7 Am Dm7 B C G7 A7 C#dim.
— Jo - nah, good - bye. How'm I — rid - in'? — I'm
Dm7(♭5) G7 C A♭ B♭7 E♭ Cm7 E♭ B♭7
rid - in' high. — Float - ing — on a
f
E♭ Cm7 E♭ B♭7
star - lit ceil - ing, Dot - ing — on the cards I'm deal - ing,
Gm7(♭5) C7 Edim. Fm Guitar tacet B7 cresc.
Gloat - ing, — be - cause I'm feel - ing so hap - hap -
mp
cresc.

G7
G
G7
mf
Cmaj. 7
C7
Cm7(♭5)
C7
- hap - py, I'm slap hap - py.
So ring bells, –
f
mf
Gm7
G7
B
G7
Cmaj. 7
C7
Cm7(♭5)
C7
Gm7
G7
sing songs, –
Blow horns, –
beat gongs, –
B
G7
E7
D
E7
Am
Dm7
Our love
nev - er will die,
B
C
G7
A7
A♭7
G7
C
1.
Dm7(♭5)
G+
2.
C
How'm I
rid - in'?
I'm rid - in' high.
f
sf

RIDIN' HIGH

PATTER

What do I care
If Missus Harrison Williams is the best
dressed woman in town?
What do I care
If Countess Barbara Hutton has a
Rolls-Royce built for each gown?
Why should I have the vapors
When I read in the papers
That Missus Simpson dined behind
the throne?
I've got a cute king of my own.
What do I care
If Katie Hepburn is famous for the world's
most beautiful nose,
Or, if I, for my sins
Don't possess underpins

Like the pegs "Legs" Dietrich shows?
I'm feeling swell,
In fact so well
It's time some noise began,
For although I'm not
A big shot,
Still, I've got my man.

SECOND PATTER

What do I care
If Missus Dorothy Parker has the country's
wittiest brain?
What do I care
If little Eleanor Jarrett only swims in
vintage champagne?
Why should I be a-flutter

When Republicans mutter
That Missus R gets pay to write her day,
If I could write my nights, hey, hey!
What do I care
If fair Tallulah possesses tons and tons of
jewels from gents?
Or, if some one observes
That I haven't the curves
That Simone Simon presents?
I'm doin' fine,
My life's divine,
I'm living in the sun
'Cause I've a big date
With my fate,
So I rate
A-1.

Copyright © 1936 by Chappell & Co., Inc.
Copyright Renewed

Sheet music cover for Cole's 1936 hit

OURS

PATTER

She: Don't say "Venice" to me,
Or suggest that old Riviera,
Those faded hot spots fill me with gloom, somehow,
As for a Hindu temple, my pet,
I wouldn't enter one on a bet.
Why I'd be afraid of being chased by a sacred cow.
Don't expect me to dream
Of the silent Sierras, dear,
Or to love that fattening cream
That they give you in Devonshire,
Don't mention the wilds of Paris,
Or, as you call it "gay Paree,"
I may not be right,
But New York is quite
Wild enough for me.

REFRAIN 2

She: Ours, the glitter of Broadway, Saturday night,
Ours, a box at the Garden, watching a fight,
Ours, the mad brouhaha of the Plaza's Persian Room,
Or, if this fills you with gloom,
We can go and admire Grant's tomb.
Ours, a home on the river facing the East,
Or on one of Park Avenue's least frightening tow'rs.
All the chat you're chattin'
Sounds to me like Latin,
Why don't we stay in Manhattan
And play it's all ours.

Copyright © 1936 by Chappell & Co., Inc.
Copyright Renewed

OURS

"Red, Hot and Blue"

Words and Music by
COLE PORTER

Copyright © 1936 by Chappell & Co., Inc.
Copyright Renewed

B♭
B♭maj. 7
Gm7
A7
Dm
A7
They've seen our cars
In front of
Dm
F
Bm 7(♮5)
Gm7(♭5)
B♭
C7
so man-y bars when we should be un-der the stars, To-geth-er, but a -
F
F
Bdim.
E♭
riten.
lone.
Ours is the chance
riten.
E♭m
F7
B♭
a tempo
to make ro-mance our own.
a tempo

B♭
Dm
B♭
Refrain With great feeling, but in a steady flowing rhythm
p-mf
Ours, the white Ri-vi-er-a, un-der the moon,
p-mf
B♭
Dm
B♭
Ours, a gon-do-la
B♭+
E♭
glid-ing on a la-goon,
Ours, a
G7
Cm7
E♭
F7
tem-ple ser-ene by the green Ar-a-bian Sea, or

Edim.
F7
molto cresc.
B♭
Gm
may - be you'd ra - ther be go - ing ga - ga in
molto cresc.
Cm7
F7
Cm7
F7
B♭
Dm7
gay Par - ee.
Ours,
p subito
B♭
F
the si - lent Si - er - ras greet-ing the dawn, -
Or a
B♭7
B♭+
E♭
sun spot - ted De - von - shire lawn dot - ted with flowers.

Cm7
mf molto espr.
Cm7(♭5)
Mine the in - cli - na - tion
mf molto espr.
B♭
E dim.
F7
B dim.
Cm7
Yours, the in - spi - ra - tion,
D7
G7
C7(9)
F7
Why don't we take a va - ca - tion and make it all
lightly and a little faster
rall. poco
1. B♭
G♭
Cm7(♭5)
F7
2. B♭
Gm7
ours.
ours.
p
L.H.
poco rit.
p
L.H.
morendo
pp

IN THE STILL OF THE NIGHT

"Rosalie"

Words and Music by
COLE PORTER

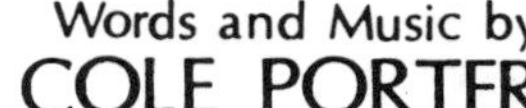

Andantino (in a steady movement, but not too fast)
Piano
mf
mp
dim.
F
Mysteriously
p
p a tempo
Fm6
In the still of the night,
F
Fm6
As I gaze from my win - dow,

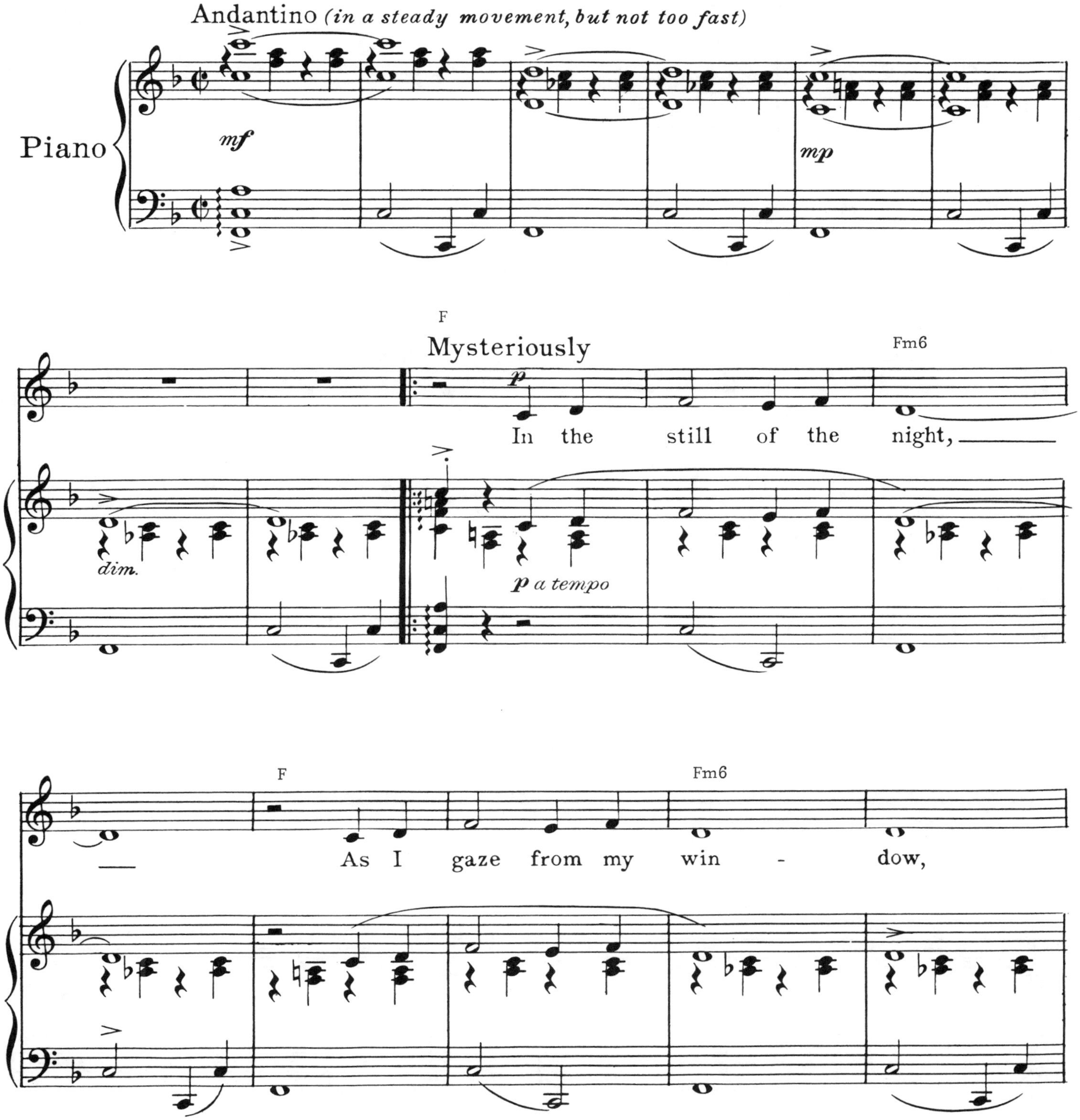

Copyright © 1937 by Chappell & Co., Inc.
Copyright Renewed

Gm7
C7
mf
F
At the moon in its flight, My thoughts all stray to
mf
Gm7
C7
F
p
you.
In the still of the
p
Fm6
F
Fm6
night,
While the world is in slum -
E7
Am
E7
molto crescendo
ber,
Oh, the times with-out num - ber, Dar-ling, when I
molto crescendo

Appassionato
mf
Am
C7
cresc.
F
f
say to you:
"Do
you love me
B♭
Gm7
C7
espressivo
As I love
you?
F
più f
F+
Are you my life - to -
be,
C7
Cm6
My dream come true?"

Am7 mf D7
Am7
D7
Gm
B♭m6
Or will this dream of mine fade
mf subito
sf
subito calmato
out of sight Like the moon, growing
F rit
p a tempo
B dim.
rit
p a tempo
dim, on the rim of the hill
C9
F
Bdim.
sempre p
in the chill, Still of the
Gm7
C

1. F
Fm6
mf
night?
mf
2. F
Fm6
F
F
mf
night?
mf
mp
Fm6
Fm6
F6
F6
p
pp
morendo
ppp

AT LONG LAST LOVE

"You Never Know"

Words and Music by
COLE PORTER

Copyright © 1938 by Chappell & Co., Inc.
Copyright Renewed

Cm
D7
G7 sus. 4
G7
love, ___ I've no sense of val - ues _ left at all. ___ Is this a
Cm
Fm
Guitar tacet
G
Fm6
G
play - time _ af-faire of May - time, Or is it a wind - fall? ___
Refrain
C
G
Am
slowly, with warm expression
p-mf
G
G7
Am
Is it an earth quake ___ or sim - ply a shock? ___
Em
F
A7
Is it the good tur - tle soup or mere - ly the

Dm Dm6 A A7
mock? Is it a cock - tail, this feel - ing of
F6 Dm6 cresc. F G7
joy, Or is what I feel the real Mc -
cresc.
C C G Am
mf mp
Coy? Is it for all time,
mf mp
G G7 Am Em
— or sim - ply a lark? Is it Gra -

C7 B♭ F♯dim. 7 E7 F6 F
mf
molto
na-da I see or on-ly As-bu-ry Park? Is it a
mf
molto
Am6 Fm C C
espressivo
fan - cy not worth think-ing of,
espressivo
Gm6 A7 D7 G7
p
cresc.
Or is it At Long Last
f
p
cresc.
1. C F6 A7 Fm G7 2. C F6 C
mf
Love. Is it a Love.
mf
mf
mf
Ped. *

FROM ALPHA TO OMEGA

"You Never Know"

Words and Music by
COLE PORTER

Copyright © 1938 by Chappell & Co., Inc.
Copyright Renewed

Cm D7 Eb Gm D7 Gm Bbm6
ev - 'ry an - gle, You're the ban - gle I long to dan - gle, For from
F Dm Db+ Dm6 G7 G7(b5) C7
base - ment_ to roof, From Wag-ner op'-ra to op'-ra bouffe,_
rall.
più rit.
C7
Refrain
in strict rhythm, but not too fast
F Dm Gm C7 F G7 Bb6
p-mf
From Al - pha_ to O - me - ga_ From A to Zee,_
B♮ dim. 7 C7 F Dm Gm C7 F G7 C7
_ From Al - pha_ to O - me - ga_ you're made for me._

D♯dim. 7 Ddim.7 C Dm Gm6 A7 Dm Gm6 Dm C
From left hooks by Demp-sey_ to Brad-dock's up-per cuts,_
G7 Cm G7 Cm Fm6 G7
From Jer-i-cho_ to Ko-ko-mo_ Not to
C7 Am Bdim. 7 C7 p F Dm
men-tion from soup to nuts;_ From Jour-nal_ un-til
p
Gm C7 F G7 B♭6 B♮dim. 7 C7 F7 poco a
Mir-ror,_ from coast to coast,_ From Jul-iet to Nor-ma
poco a

G♯dim. 7 F7
poco cresc.
B♭
C♯ dim. 7
B♭6
Shear - er_ You're what I like the most._ And from
poco cresc.
f
mf
Bdim. 7
F6 E F
morn - ing_ un - til eve - ning_ In mis - 'ry I shall pine,_
Cm6 D7 G7 C7(9) C7(♭9)
_ 'Til from Al - pha_ to O - me - ga_ you're
1. F F6 B♭6 C7
mf
mine._ From
mf
2. F B♭6 B♭m6 F
mine._
mf

Rex O'Malley, Clifton Webb, Lupe Velez, Libby Holman in YOU NEVER KNOW (1938)

FROM ALPHA TO OMEGA

REFRAIN 1

From Alpha to Omega,
From A to Z,
From Alpha to Omega,
You're made for me.
From left hooks by Dempsey to Braddock's upper-cuts,
From Jericho to Kokomo, not to mention from soup to nuts,
From Journal until Mirror,
From coast to coast,
From Juliet to Norma Shearer,
You're what I like the most,
And from morning until evening
In mis'ry I shall pine,
Till from Alpha to Omega you're mine.

REFRAIN 2

From Alpha to Omega,
From A to Z,
From Alpha to Omega,
You're made for me.
From love songs by Schumann to hits by Jerry Kern,
From Sarawak to Hackensack, not to mention,
from stem to stern,
From dyah Missus Pat Campbell
To sweet Mae West,
You happen to be the mammal
This body loves the best,
And from morning until evening,
Will you stun yourself with wine?
Certainly, till from Alpha to Omega you're mine.

REFRAIN 3

From Alpha to Omega,
From A to Z,
From Alpha to Omega,
You're made for me.
From Lou Gehrig's home-run to Lou Chiozza's bunt,
From Tripoli to Kankakee, not to mention from
Lynn to Lunt,
From great eighty-pound codfish
To sardines canned,
You happen to be the odd fish
This lad would love to land,
And will you woo me and pursue me,
With sinker, hook, and line?
Yes, till from Alpha to Omega you're mine.
And will you chase me,
And embrace me,
And say that I'm divine?
Till from Alpha to Omega you're mine.

REFRAIN 4

From Alpha to Omega,
From A to Z,
From Alpha to Omega,
You're made for me.
From cotton ploughed under
To this year's bumper crop,
From Benzedrine
To Ovaltine,
Not to mention from go to stop.
From corn muffins to Triscuit
From fat to thin,
From Zev to the young Seabiscuit,
I'll bet on you to win.
And will you brunch me,
And then lunch me,
Then make me stay to dine?
Yes, till from Alpha to Omega you're mine

REFRAIN 5

From Alpha to Omega,
From A to Z,
From Alpha to Omega,
You're made for me.
From old English Sherry
To very French Vermouth,
From Mozambique
To Battle Creek,
Not to mention from North to South.*
From great eagles to sparrows,
From large to small,
From Austins to big Pierce-Arrows,
Your rumble tops 'em all,
And will you beat me
And maltreat me,
And bend my Spanish spine?
Yes, till from Alpha to Omega you're mine.

*From COLE Note: Mr. Webb, go Southern, and pronounce this Nauth and Sooth.

Finale
ACT II

From Martinis to brandy,
From East to West,
From Salomey to Sally Randy,
I like your fan the best,
And from morning until ev'ning,
The sun will never shine
Till from Alpha to Omega you're mine.

Copyright © 1938 by Chappell & Co., Inc.
Copyright Renewed

FAR AWAY

"Leave It To Me"

Words and Music by
COLE PORTER

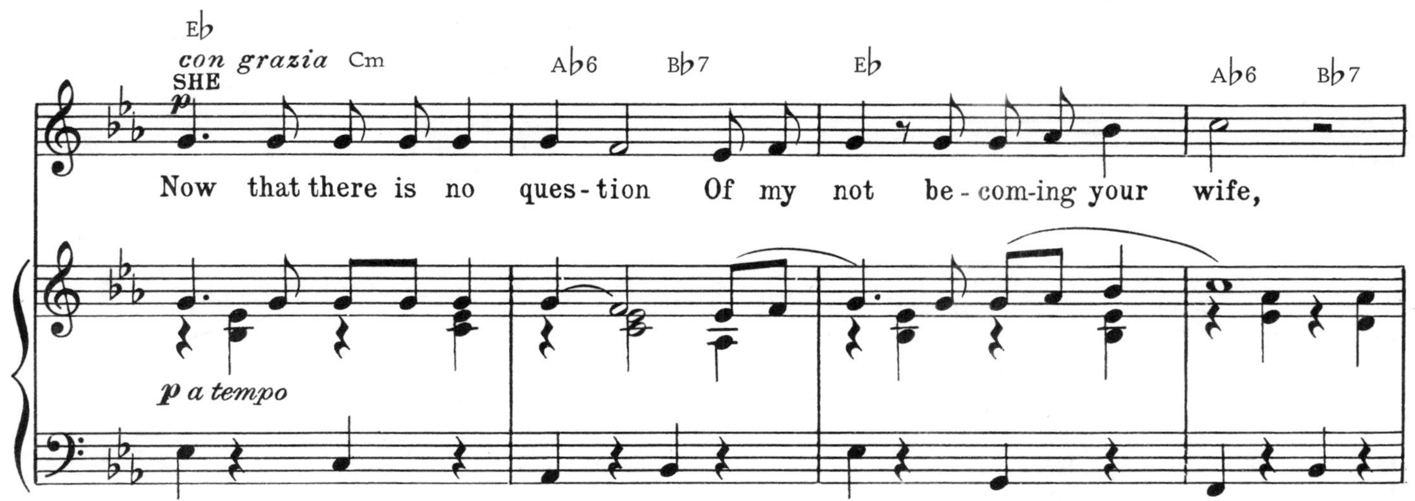

Copyright © 1938 by Chappell & Co., Inc.
Copyright Renewed

E♭7
A♭
A♭6
B♭7
HE
If you on-ly ac-cept it I shall prove my gra-ti-tude. Go
E♭
E♭6
E♭
E♭maj7
E♭7
E♭7
A♭6
A♭m6
B♭7
E♭
on, spring it, If pos-si-ble, sing it For I'm in a lyr-i-cal mood.
Refrain
Guitar tacet
Fm
p-mf
Fm6
E♭6
E♭
Fm
D dim. 7
1. I'm not sug-gest-ing to you A draft-y cot-tage for
2. (I'm not sug)-gest-ing we get A tent a-top of Thi-
p-mf
E♭6
E♭
F7
B♭7
E♭
E♭m
two By the side of a wide wa-ter-fall,
bet, Or that we cross the sea in a yawl,

B♭7 Cm6 B♭7 E♭ C7 Fm
But you must grant me, sweet-heart, That it would be rath-er smart
But, dear, with me as your mate You'll a-gree it would be great
A♭m6 E♭ F♯dim. 7 E♭ F7 A♭6 A♭m6
Guitar tacet
To get a-way, Far a-way from it all.
To get a-way, Far a-way from it all.
B♭7 Fm Fm6 E♭6 E♭ Fm G7
p
I'm not pro-pos-ing we lease A tum-bling tem-ple in
I don't sug-gest that we test The o-pen spac-es out
p
C7 F7 B♭7 E♭ E♭m
Greece, Or a hole in the "ole" Chi-na wall,
West, In a shack with no back to the hall,

B♭7 Cm6 B♭7 E♭ C7 Fm
But when it's all said and done, I'll ad - mit it would be fun
But if we took some nice nook I could watch you while you cook,
mf
A♭m6 Guitar tacet E♭ G7(♭5) C7 Fm B♭7 E♭
To get a - way, Far a - way from it all.
And get a - way, Far a - way from it all.
Guitar tacet D♭6 D E♭7 A♭ Bdim. 7
mf
What a joy not to fear As we wan - der 'neath the
With the blue skies a - bove, And a peace-ful ha - bi -
mf
A♭6 A♭ C7(♭5) F7 E♭ A♭m F7 B♭ E♭m6 F7
moon, That some ra - di - o near Will re - peat that Ber-lin tune.
tat, There'll be no dan - ger of Hear-ing Frank-lin give a chat.

B♭ Cm6 B♭7 E♭ C7 Fm
mf
— And to be cer - tain, my dear, That the read-ers of Hey-wood Broun—
— And we'll know al - so, my love, Gro - ver Whe - lan and his hat—
A♭m6 Guitar tacet E♭ Cm E♭ F7
— Are far a - way, Far, far a - way,
— Are far a - way, Far, far a - way,
A dim. 7 E♭ E♭6 F7 B♭7
f
— 1.-2.But me from you — Nev - er too — far a - way.—
1. E♭ Guitar tacet 2. E♭ E♭6 E♭
2.I'm not sug -
mf
f

GET OUT OF TOWN

"Leave It To Me"

Words and Music by
COLE PORTER

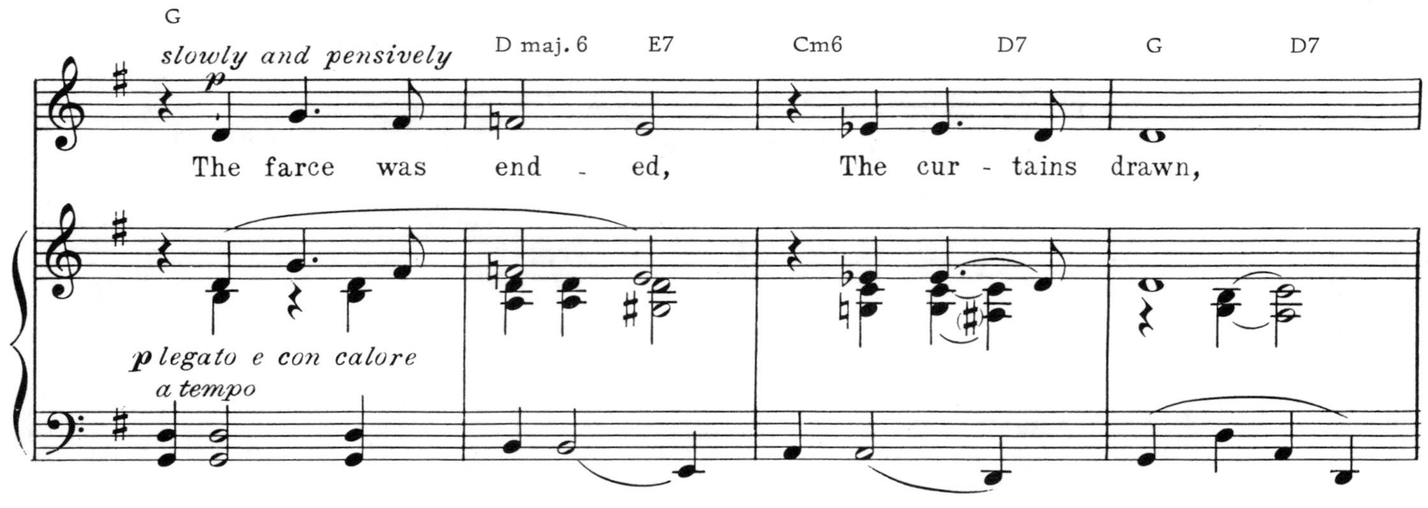

Copyright © 1938 by Chappell & Co., Inc.
Copyright Renewed

D7
B dim. 7
Am
C6
B7 sus. 4
B7
mf
p
But now from no - where you come to me as be - fore To
mf più espr.
p
Em
Em
C7
C♯dim. 7
D
D7(♭9)
take my heart and break my heart once more.
f molto espr. e rall.
Gm
Refrain
in steady slow tempo, with increasing expression
p a tempo
Gm6
Get out of town Be - fore it's too late, my love;
p a tempo
Gm
p
Get out of town, Be good to me, please.
mf
p

B♭maj. 7
B♭6
mf
Gm6
F7
F6
Why wish me harm?
Why not re - tire to a farm
f
mf
E♮ dim. 7
E♭6
A
And be con - tent - ed to charm
The birds off the
D
D7
G
p
trees?
Just dis-ap-pear,
I care for you
p
Gm6
Gm
mp
poco a poco
much too much,
And when you are near,
mf
mp
poco a poco

cresc.
D
Gm
Fm6
G7
mf
Close to me, dear, We touch too much. The
cresc.
f
mf
Cm
E♭m
E♭m6
B♭
Guitar tacet
thrill when we meet Is so bit-ter sweet That, dar-ling, it's get-ting me down.
legato
pensively
Fm6
E♭+
G7
Cm
E♭m6
F7
mf
f
mp
So on your mark, get set, Get out of
mf
f appassionato
sf
mp softly
1.
B♭
F♯dim. 7
D7(♭9)
2.
B♭
town.
town.
mf
mf
espr

MOST GENTLEMEN DONT LIKE LOVE

"Leave It To Me"

Words and Music by
COLE PORTER

Copyright © 1938 by Chappell & Co., Inc.
Copyright Renewed

D7
mosso (lighter)
G G D7 G Em G
now that Mum-my's more ma-ture And knows her way a-bout, She
D7 G E7 C6 rall. D7 G7
does-n't b'lieve in "Vive l'a-mour" For Mum-my's found out:
rall.
Refrain
C F Dm B7(♮5) E7 A7 F6
Slowly, but rhythmically
p-mf
Most gen-tle-men don't like love, They just like to
p-mf
B♭7 A♭7 G7 C F6 C A♭7 E♭m6 A♭7 C F
kick it a-round; Most gen-
R.H.

Dm B7(♮5) E7 A7 F6
-tle-men can't take love, 'Cause most gen-tle-men
B♭7 A♭7 G7 C Fm 6 C D♯dim. 7 C+ Am
mf
can't be pro-found. As mad-am Sapph-o
R.H.
mf
C6 B7 D♯dim. 7 E7 f A7
in some son-net said: "A slap and a tick-le Is
f
A♭7 G7 Guitar tacet G G+ C F
mp
all that the fick-le male Ev-er has in his head." For most gen-
mp

Dm B7(♮5) E7 A7 F6 Fm6 G7 D# dim. 7
poco a poco cresc.
tle - men don't like love. I've been in love So
poco a poco cresc.
C A♭7 F6 E7 Am C6 G6 Am6 Fm6
f
I know what I'm talk - ing of; And oh, to my woe I have found
f
C G+ Gm A7 A♭7 F6 B♭7 A♭7 G7 C
mp
They just like to kick it a - round.
mp
1. D♯dim. 7 C D7 G7 sus. 4 G7
f
2. A♭9 C
f

MOST GENTLEMEN DON'T LIKE LOVE

REFRAIN 2

Most gentlemen don't like love, they just like
to kick it around,
Most gentlemen don't like love, 'cause most gentlemen
can't be profound.
So just remember when you get that glance,
A romp and a quickie
Is all little Dickie
Means
When he mentions romance,
For most gentlemen don't like love,
They just like to kick it around.

REFRAIN 3

Most gentlemen don't like love, they just like
to kick it around,
Most gentlemen don't like love, 'cause most gentlemen
can't be profound.
In ev'ry land, children, they're all the same,
A pounce in the clover
And then when it's over
"So long and what is your name?"
'Cause most gentlemen don't like love,
They just like to kick it around.

REFRAIN 4

Most gentlemen don't like love, they just like
to kick it around,
Most gentlemen don't like love, 'cause most gentlemen
can't be profound.
So if your boy friend, some fine night, should say
He'll love you forever
And part from you never,
Just push him out of the hay, (way)
'Cause most gentlemen don't like love,
They just like to kick it around.

Copyright © 1938 by Chappell & Co., Inc.
Copyright Renewed

Mary Martin sings MY HEART BELONGS TO DADDY as Gene Kelly and cast look on in LEAVE IT TO ME (1938)

MY HEART BELONGS TO DADDY

REFRAIN 2

Saint Patrick's day,
Although I may
Be seen wearing green with a paddy,
I'm always sharp
When playing the harp,
'Cause my heart belongs to Daddy.
Though other dames
At football games
May long for a strong undergraddy,
I never dream
Of making the team
'Cause my heart belongs to Daddy.
Yes, my heart belongs to Daddy,
So I simply couldn't be bad.
Yes, my heart belongs to Daddy,
Da-da, da-da-da, da-da-da, dad!
So I want to warn you, laddie,
Tho' I simply hate to be frank,
That I can't be mean to Daddy
'Cause my Da-da-da-daddy might spank.
In matters artistic
He's not modernistic
So Da-da-da-daddy might spank.

Copyright © 1938 by Chappell & Co., Inc.
Copyright Renewed

MY HEART BELONGS TO DADDY

"Leave It To Me"

Words and Music by
COLE PORTER

Copyright © 1938 by Chappell & Co., Inc.
Copyright Renewed

G7
C
Ab7
G7
C
Bb7
To keep my mind On my dut-ies. For
mf
p
Eb
Bb7
Eb
Bb7
Cm
Fm
G7
since I came to care For such a sweet mil-lion-aire.
dolce
poco rit.
G7+
Cm
Refrain (slow Rhumba tempo)
While tear-ing off A game of golf I may make a play for the
mp
Fm6
G7
Fm
A7
Gm
G7
cad-dy; But when I do I don't fol-low through 'Cause my heart be-longs to

Cm
G7+
Cm
Dad-dy. If I in-vite A boy some night To
Cm
Fm6
G7
dine on my fine fin-nan had-die, I just a-dore His
Fm A7 Gm G7 Cm
ask-ing for more, But my heart be-longs to Dad-dy. Yes, my
mf più
Cm
G7
heart be-longs to Dad-dy, So I sim-ply could-n't be bad. Yes, my
espressivo

G7
C
heart be-longs_ to Dad-dy, Da-da, da-da-da, da-da-da - ad! So I
3
G7
C
C7
want to warn_ you, lad-die, Tho' I know you're per - fect - ly
F
Fm
C
swell, That my heart be - longs_ to Dad-dy_ 'Cause my
Fm6
G7
1. Cm
G7+
2. Cm
Dad-dy, he treats it so well. While well._
rall.
a tempo
mf
sf

BETWEEN YOU AND ME

"Broadway Melody of 1940"

Words and Music by
COLE PORTER

Copyright © 1939 by Chappell & Co., Inc.
Copyright Renewed

Am Dm6 Am F6 G7 C B♭ C7
rall.
near you seem, At night when I dream,-But when I wak - en, How far!
rall.
F
Refrain (slowly and with warmth)
p a tempo
B♮dim. 7 Gm
Be - tween you and me, You're some - thing spec -
p a tempo
B♭m F B♮dim. 7 F D♭7
cresc.
tac - u - lar, Be - tween you and me, You're a
cresc.
F6 F Cm6
prize. Be - tween you and
mf
espr.

D7
Gm
B♭6
C
F♭
C7
me, To use — the ver - nac - u - lar, —
F
Fmaj. 7
F7
D7
G7
You've got what they call "Oomph" in your eyes. —
3
3
3
p subito
f
C7(9)
F
p
B♮dim. 7
Till I make you mine
p
Gm
B♭m
F
cresc.
Your heart — I'll bom - bard to get, — No mat - ter how
cresc.

E7
A
A7
hard to get — it may be.
mf
D7
molto espr.
G7
D♭7
F
p
So why not com - bine
And chuck_the for -
molto espr.
sf
p
Cm6
D7
G7
C7
mf rall.
mal - i - ty
Be - tween love and
be - tween you and
mf rall.
1. F
a tempo
B♮dim. 7
G7
C7
2. F
B♮dim. 7
F
me.
me.
a tempo
mf
f
p

Eleanor Powell and Fred Astaire dance the "Beguine" in the film BROADWAY MELODY OF 1940

I CONCENTRATE ON YOU

"Broadway Melody of 1940"

Words and Music by
COLE PORTER

Copyright © 1939 by Chappell & Co., Inc.
Copyright Renewed

B♭7
E♭m6
B♭7
A♭m
E♭m
F7
G♭7
When-ev-er the win-ter-winds be-come too strong,
F7
B♭7(+5) B♭7
E♭
A♭6
I con-cen-trate on you.
E♭
E♭maj. 7
E♭6
B♭+
When for-tune cries "nay, nay!" to me
mf
E♭m
G♭9
G♭7
C♭6
And peo-ple de-clare "You're through,"

D♭7 E♭m7 E♭dim. D♭7 C♭ G♭ G♭dim. G♭
When-ev-er the Blues be-come My on-ly song,
F7 F7(♭5) B♮+ B♭+ B♭7 E♭ A♭6 E♭ Tacet
I con-cen-trate on you. On your
mf
F7 B♮dim. E♭+ E♭
smile so sweet, so ten-der, When at
espressivo
espr.
A♭6 B♭7 Gm B♭+ E♭ Gm E♭7 Tacet
first {my {your kiss {you {I de-cline, On the

A♭
D♭7
C♭
G♭
light in your eyes, When {you / I} sur - ren - der And once a -
cresc.
E♭m6
F7
B♭
B♭maj. 7
B♭7
gain our arms in - ter - twine.
f
con sforza
E♭
Gm
Cm6
And so when wise men say to me
f passionately
più f
B♭9
B♮dim
B♭9
E♭
G7
G7sus E♭
G7
That love's young dream nev - er comes true,
mf

Bbm6 C7+5 C7 Fm C Fm
To prove that ev - en wise men can be wrong,
mf calmato
poco rit.
F7 F7b5 Bb7(+5) Bb7 Eb 1. Ab6 Eb Bb7
I con - cen - trate on you.
p poco allarg.
2. Ab6 Eb Fm Bb13(9b)
I con - cen-trate, and con - cen-trate
a tempo
pp
Bb7 Bb6 Eb
on you.
morendo
8

BUT IN THE MORNING, NO

"DuBarry Was A Lady"

Words and Music by
COLE PORTER

Copyright © 1939 by Chappell & Co., Inc.
Copyright Renewed

A7 Dm6 A Dm Fm C G7
You run mine and I run Fran - ce's, So there's on- ly one ques - tion that's
C C♯dim. 7 A7 Dm F C C Gm6 A
hot, Will we have fun or not?
mf
Refrain F6
Slow Tempo di Gavotte (with precision)
G7 G7 C C
She: Are you fond of rid - ing dear? Kind - ly tell me if
p staccato and gracefully
F G7 Dm6 E7 E7
so. He: Yes, I'm fond of rid - ing, dear,

Am mf E7 Am F7(♭5) Am p F6
But in the morn - ing, no! She: Are you good at
mf with slight swing
f
p staccato and gracefully
G7 G7 C C F G7 Dm6
shoot - ing, dear? Kind - ly tell me if so. He: Yes, I'm good at
E7 E7 Am mf E7 Am mp F6 G7 C E
Con grandezza
shoot - ing, dear, But in the morn - ing, no! When the dawn's ear - ly
mf with slight swing
mp legato e poco espr.
Am Dm C♯dim. 7 Dm F6 G7 C Am
light comes to cru - ci - fy my night, That's the time When

G D7 G A7 F6
I'm in low. She: Are you fond of
f sff p staccato and gracefully
G7 G7 C C F G7 Dm6
box - ing dear? Kind - ly tell me if so. He: Yes I'm fond of
E7 E7 Am E7 Am Dm6
box - ing dear, But in the morn - ing, no, no, no, no,
mf f deciso e marcatissimo
Am Dm Am E7 1. A 2. A
no, no, no, no, no! no!
marcato sf

BUT IN THE MORNING, NO

REFRAIN 2

He: Do you like the mountains, dear?
Kindly tell me, if so.
She: Yes, I like the mountains, dear,
But in the morning, no
He: Are you good at climbing, dear?
Kindly tell me, if so.
She: Yes, I'm good at climbing, dear,
But in the morning, no.
When the light of the day
Comes and drags me from the hay,
That's the time
When I'm
In low.
He: Have you tried Pike's Peak, my dear?
Kindly tell me, if so.
She: Yes, I've tried Pike's Peak, my dear,
But in the morning, no, no—no, no,
No, no, no, no, no!

REFRAIN 3

She: Are you fond of swimming, dear?
Kindly tell me, if so.
He: Yes, I'm fond of swimming, dear,
But in the morning, no.
She: Can you do the crawl, my dear?
Kindly tell me, if so.
He: I can do the crawl, my dear,
But in the morning, no.
When the sun through the blind
Starts to burn my poor behind
That's the time
When I'm
In low.
She: Do you use the breast stroke, dear?
Kindly tell me, if so.
He: Yes, I use the breast stroke, dear,
But in the morning, no, no—no, no,
No, no, no, no, no!

REFRAIN 4

He: Are you fond of Hot Springs, dear?
Kindly tell me, if so.
She: Yes, I'm fond of Hot Springs, dear,
But in the morning, no.
He: D'you like old Point Comfort, dear?
Kindly tell me, if so.
She: I like old Point Comfort, dear,
But in the morning, no.
When my maid toddles in
With my orange juice and gin,
That's the time
When I'm
In low.
He: Do you like Mi-ami, dear?
Kindly tell me, if so.
She: Yes, I like your-ami, dear,
But in the morning, no, no—no, no,
No, no, no, no, no!

NOTE: To satisfy the objections of some of the critics as well as the complaints of the Boston censors, Cole wrote the next two refrains:

REFRAIN 5

She: Are you good at football, dear?
Kindly tell me, if so.
He: Yes, I'm good at football, dear,
But in the morning, no.
She: Do you ever fumble, dear?
Kindly tell me, if so.
He: No, I never fumble, dear,
But in the morning, yes.
When I start with a frown
Reading Winchell upside down,
That's the time
When I'm
In low.
She: Do you like a scrimmage, dear?
Kindly tell me, if so.
He: Yes, I like a scrimmage, dear,
But in the morning, no, no—no, no,
No, no, no no, no!

REFRAIN 6

He: D'you like Nelson Eddy, dear?
Kindly tell me, if so.
She: I like Nelson Eddy, dear,
But in the morning, no.
He: D'you like Tommy Manville, dear?
Kindly tell me, if so.
She: I like Tommy Manville, dear,
But in the morning, no.
When my maid says, "Madame!
Wake 'em and make 'em scram,"
That's the time
When I'm
In low.
He: Are you fond of Harvard men?
Kindly tell me, if so.
She: Yes, I'm fond of Harvard men,
But in the morning, no, no—no, no,
No, no, no, no, no!

REFRAIN 7

She: Are you good at figures, dear?
Kindly tell me, if so.
He: Yes, I'm good at figures dear,
But in the morning, no.
She: D'you do double entry, dear?
Kindly tell me, if so.
He: I do double entry, dear,
But in the morning, no
When the sun on the rise
Shows the bags beneath my eyes.
That's the time
When I'm
In low.
She: Are you fond of business, dear?
Kindly tell me, if so.
He: Yes, I'm fond of business, dear,
But in the morning, no, no—no, no,
No, no, no, no, no!

REFRAIN 8

He: Are you in the market, dear?
Kindly tell me, if so.
She: Yes, I'm in the market, dear,
But in the morning, no.
He: Are you fond of bulls and bears?
Kindly tell me, if so.
She: Yes, I'm fond of bears and bulls,
But in the morning, no.
When I'm waked by my fat
Old canary, singing flat,
That's the time
When I'm
In low.
He: Would you ever sell your seat?
Kindly tell me, if so.
She: Yes, I'd gladly sell my seat,
But in the morning, no, no—no, no,
No, no, no, no, no!

REFRAIN 9

She: Are you fond of poker, dear?
Kindly tell me, if so.
He: Yes, I'm fond of poker, dear,
But in the morning, no.
She: Do you ante up, my dear?
Kindly tell me, if so.
He: Yes, I ante up-my dear,
But in the morning, no.
When my old Gunga Din
Brings the Bromo Seltzer in,
That's the time
When I'm
In low.
She: Can you fill an inside straight?
Kindly tell me, if so.
He: I've filled plenty inside straight,
But in the morning, no, no—no, no,
No, no, no, no, no!

REFRAIN 10

He: Are you fond of Democrats?
Kindly tell me, if so.
She: Yes, I'm fond of Democrats,
But in the morning, no.
He: Do you like Republicans?
Kindly tell me, if so.
She: Yes, I like Republi-cans,
But in the morning, no.
When my pet pekinese
Starts to cross his Q's and P's,
That's the time
When I'm
In low.
He: Do you like third parties, dear?
Kindly tell me, if so.
She: Yes, I love third parties, dear,
But in the morning, no, no—no, no,
No, no, no, no, no!

Copyright © 1939
by Chappell & Co., Inc.
Copyright Renewed

DO I LOVE YOU?

"DuBarry Was A Lady"

Words and Music by
COLE PORTER

Copyright © 1939 by Chappell & Co., Inc.
Copyright Renewed

G7 G7 G♯dim. 7 Am C6 Am6 D7
you, I com-posed a tune, So will you lis-ten to it,
F♯dim. 7 C A7 D7 G7 C Am F6
dear?
G7
Refrain
Moderato (in steady rhythm, without dragging)
C Gm6 A7(-9) A7
p-mf
Do I love you, do I? Does-n't
p-mf
Dm F+ F6 G7 F G7 C
one and one make two? Do I love

Gm6
A7(-9)
D7
Bm
D
G7
you, do I? Does Ju - ly need a sky of blue?
F
G7
G7
C
G7
G7
C
C
Would I miss you, would I,
C
G7
C7
F
Fm
F
G7
F
C9
C
Guitar tacet
If you ev - er should go a - way? If the
A m
B♭
C7
F
C♯dim. 7
B♭7(♭5)
A7
A7
sun should de - sert the day, What would life be?

G7
Dm
G7(9)
Guitar tacet
C
mp
Gm
Will I leave you,
R.H.
mp
A7(-9)
A7
Dm
F+
F6
G7
F
nev- er? Could the o - cean leave the shore?
G7
C
Gm6
A7(-9)
Will I wor - ship you for - ev - er? Is - n't
D7
Bm
D
G7
F6
G7
G7
C
mp
poco a poco
heav - en for - ev - er more? Do I love
mp
poco a poco

G7 G7 C C7 F E F
cresc.
mf
you, do I? Oh, my dear, it's so
mf
G G♭ F Fm6 D7(♭5) C C+
eas - y to see, Don't you know I do? Don't I
Am C7 Am6 A♭+ G7
poco allarg.
show you I do, Just as you love
poco allarg.
1. C Am C+ G7
Guitar tacet
mf
me? Do I
marcato
mf
2. C Am C+ C C6
me?
f
sf

KATIE WENT TO HAITI

"DuBarry Was A Lady"

Words and Music by
COLE PORTER

Copyright © 1939 by Chappell & Co., Inc.
Copyright Renewed

C6 C C C♯dim. 7 F6 G7
p
Af - ter a week in Hai - ti She
f R.H.
p
C C6 A7 D7 G7 G7 C E7 Am
start - ed to go a - way, Then Ka - tie met an - oth - er
C6 D7 C C F maj. 7 G7 C C6 C
na - tie, So Ka - tie pro - longed her stay.
C6 C C7 C7(9) C7 F C7(9)
mf
Af - ter a month in Hai - ti
f R.H.
mf

Am
C7
C7(9)
Am
F6
G7(sus 4)
G7(9)
— She de - cid - ed to re - sume her trip, But
C
E7
Am
C6
D7
C
C
Ka - tie met still an - oth - er na - tie, — And Ka - tie
Fmaj. 7
G7
C
C6
C
C6
C
G7
missed the ship. So
mf
f
R.H.
mf
C6
F6
G7(sus. 4)
G7
C6
Ka - tie — lived in Hai - ti, — Her life there,

D7 G7(sus. 4) F6 G7(sus. 4) G7 F C7
it was great, 'Cause Ka - tie knew her
F6 Fm6 C C6 f E7 A7 D7
Hai - ti And prac - ti - cal - ly all Hai-
G7 1. C C6 C C6 C
- ti knew Ka - tie.
R.H.
2. C C6 C C6 C C
Ka - tie.
R.H.
ff
sf

FRIENDSHIP

"DuBarry Was A Lady"

Words and Music by
COLE PORTER

Copyright © 1939 by Chappell & Co., Inc.
Copyright Renewed

D Dm E7 Dm7 C G7
hap - py you land in jail, I'm your bail. It's
teeth and you're out to dine, Bor - row mine. It's
f
C G7
friend - ship, friend - ship, Just a per - fect blend - ship. When
friend - ship, friend - ship, Just a per - fect blend - ship. When
C G7 C7 F Fm D7♭5 C Fm6 C A♭7 G7 C
oth - er friend - ships have been for - got Ours will still be hot. Lah - dle -
oth - er friend - ships have been for - gate Ours will still be great. Lah - dle -
mf
D D♭ 1. C 2. C
ah - dle - ah - dle, dig, dig, dig. 2. If you're 3. If they
ah - dle - ah - dle, chuck, chuck, chuck.
mp
mp

C D7 G7 C
ev - er black your eyes, Put me wise.
mf
C7 F G7
If they ev - er cook your goose, Turn me loose.
C G
If they ev - er put a
mf
D Dm E7 Dm7 C G7
bul - let through your brrr - ain, I'll com - plain. It's
f

C
friend - ship, friend - ship, Just a per - fect
G7 C G7 C7
blend - ship. When oth - er friend - ships have
F Fm D7(♭5) C Fm6 C A♭7 G7 C
been for - git Ours will still be it, Lah - dle -
mf
D D♭ 1. C 2. C
ah - dle - ah - dle, hep, hep, hep. If they
mp
sf

KATIE WENT TO HAITI

REFRAIN 2

Katie stayed in Haiti
Spending all her pay.
Katie met a natie
Ev'ry other day.
Katie would tell the natie
That Katie was out for thrills
Each natie got a few for Katie
And Katie, she got the bills.
After a year in Haiti
She decided she should really go
But Katie had lived at such a ratie
That Katie had no dough
So Katie stuck to Haiti
Delighted with her fate
'Cause Katie still had Haiti
And practically all Haiti had Katie.

REFRAIN 3

Katie looked at Haiti
Feeling rather tired.
Katie met a natie
Katie was inspired.
After another natie
She sat down and wrote a book,
A guide-book for visitors to Haiti
Called "Listen, Stop, and Look!"
After the book by Katie
Had been published in the USA
The ratie of tourist trade in Haiti
Got bigger ev'ry day.
When Katie died at eighty
They buried her in state
For Katie made her Haiti
And practically all Haiti made Katie.

Copyright © 1939 by Chappell & Co., Inc.
Copyright Renewed

FRIENDSHIP

Cole Porter's original version

REFRAIN 1

He: If you're ever in a jam, here I am.
She: If you ever need a pal, I'm your gal.
He: If you ever feel so happy you land in jail,
I'm your bail.
Both: It's friendship, friendship,
Just a perfect blendship,
When other friendships have been forgot,
Ours will still be hot.
Lahdle—ahdle——dig, dig, dig.

REFRAIN 2

She: If you ever lose your way, come to May.
He: If you ever make a flop, call for Pop.
She: If you ever take a boat and get lost at sea,
Write to me.
Both: It's friendship, friendship,
Just a perfect blendship.
When other friendships have been forgit,
Ours will still be it,
Lahdle—ahdle—ahdle—chuck, chuck, chuck.

REFRAIN 3

He: If you're ever down a well, ring my bell.
She: If you ever catch on fire, send a wire.
He: If you ever lose your teeth and you're out to dine,
Borrow mine.
Both: It's friendship, friendship,
Just a perfect blendship,
When other friendships have ceased to jell
Ours will still be swell.
Lahdle—ahdle—ahdle—hep, hep, hep.

REFRAIN 4

She: If they ever black your eyes, put me wise.
He: If they ever cook your goose, turn me loose.
She: If they ever put a bullet through your brr-ain,
I'll complain.
Both: It's friendship, friendship,
Just a perfect blendship.
When other friendships go up in smoke
Ours will still be oke.
Lahdle—ahdle—ahdle—chuck, chuck, chuck.
Gong, gong, gong,
Cluck, cluck, cluck,
Woof, woof, woof,
Peck, peck, peck,
Put, put, put,
Hip, hip, hip.
Quack, quack, quack,
Tweet, tweet, tweet,
Push, push, push,
Give, give, give.

REFRAIN 5

He: If you ever lose your mind, I'll be kind.
She: If you ever lose your shirt, I'll be hurt.
He: If you're ever in a mill and get sawed in half,
I won't laugh.
Both: It's friendship, friendship,
Just a perfect blendship,
When other friendships have been forgate,
Ours will still be great.
Lahdle—ahdle—ahdle—goof, goof, goof.

REFRAIN 6

She: If they ever hang you, pard, send a card.
He: If they ever cut your throat, write a note.
She: If they ever make a cannibal stew of you,
Invite me too.
Both: It's friendship, friendship,
Just a perfect blendship,
When other friendships are up the crick,
Ours will still be slick,
Lahdle—ahdle—ahdle—zip, zip, zip.

Copyright © 1939 by Chappell & Co., Inc.
Copyright Renewed

WELL, DID YOU EVAH?

"DuBarry Was A Lady"

Words and Music by
COLE PORTER

Copyright © 1940 by Chappell & Co., Inc.
Copyright Renewed

A7 Dm Fm C G♯dim. Am D7
aw - ful, some-thing grave, And I'll show you how a Rac-quet Club_
Fm6 G7 C B♭6 C6 B♭maj. 7 C7
lad Would be - have:
poco rit
Refrain
F
Tempo di Polka
B♮dim. 7 C7
p-mf
She: Have you heard? The Coast of Maine Just got hit by a
p-mf a tempo
F Cm D7 Gm G7♭5
mf mp
hur - ri - cane? He: Well, did you e - vah! What a
mf molto marcato
mp

F Dm6 B7 C7 F
swell par - ty this is! She: Have you heard that
B♮ dim. 7 C7 F
poor dear Blanche Got run down by an a - va - lanche?
Cm D7 Gm G7♭5 F G7 C7 F
He: Well, did you e - vah! What a swell par - ty this is! What
D♭ A♭7 D♭
Dai - quir - is! What Sher - ry, please! What

E♮ dim. 7
A♭7
D♭
Bur - gun - dy! What great Pom - mer - y! What
Edim. 7
A♭7
D♭
bran - dy, wow! What whis - key, here's how! What
B♭m
Fm
G7
f
C
gin and what beer! She: Will you so - ber up, my dear?
f
F
B♮ dim. 7
C7
p
Have you heard Pro - fes - sor Munch Ate his wife and di -
p

F Cm D7 Gm G7♭5
mf mp
vorced his lunch? He: Well, did you e - vah! What a
mf molto marcato
mp
F Dm6 B7 C7 F B♮ dim. 7
swell par - ty this is! She: Mis - sus Smith in her new Hup
C7 F Cm D7 Gm G7♭5
mf mp
Crossed the bridge when the bridge was up. He: Well did you e - vah! What a
mf molto marcato
mp
1. F G7 C7 F Dm C7
swell par - ty this is!
2. F G7 C7 F
swell par - ty this is!
sf

WELL, DID YOU EVAH?

REFRAIN 1

She: Have you heard the coast of Maine
Just got hit by a hurricane?
He: Well, did you evah! What a swell party this is.
She: Have you heard that poor, dear Blanche
Got run down by an avalanche?
He: Well, did you evah! What a swell party this is.
It's great, it's grand.
It's Wonderland!
It's tops, it's first.
It's DuPont, it's Hearst!
What soup, what fish.
That meat, what a dish!
What salad, what cheese!
She: Pardon me one moment, please,
Have you heard that Uncle Newt
Forgot to open his parachute?
He: Well, did you evah! What a swell party this is.
She: Old Aunt Susie just came back
With her child and the child is black.
He: Well, did you evah! What a swell party this is.

REFRAIN 2

He: Have you heard it's in the stars
Next July we collide with Mars?
She: Well, did you evah! What a swell party this is.
He: Have you heard that Grandma Doyle
Thought the Flit was her mineral oil?
She: Well, did you evah! What a swell party this is.
What Daiquiris!
What Sherry! Please!
What Burgundy!
What great Pommery!
What brandy, wow!
What whiskey, here's how!
What gin and what beer!
He: Will you sober up, my dear?
Have you heard Professor Munch
Ate his wife and divorced his lunch?
She: Well, did you evah! What a swell party this is.
He: Have you heard that Mimmsie Starr
Just got pinched in the Astor Bar?
She: Well, did you evah! What a swell party this is!

REFRAIN 3

She: Have you heard that poor old Ted
Just turned up in an oyster bed?
He: Well, did you evah! What a swell party this is.
She: Lilly Lane has louzy luck,
She was there when the light'ning struck.
He: Well, did you evah! What a swell party this is.
It's fun, it's fine,
It's too divine.
It's smooth, it's smart.
It's Rodgers, it's Hart!
What debs, what stags.
What gossip, what gags!
What feathers, what fuss!
She: Just between the two of us,
Reggie's rather scatterbrained,
He dove in when the pool was drained.
He: Well, did you evah! What a swell party this is.
She: Mrs. Smith in her new Hup
Crossed the bridge when the bridge was up.
He: Well, did you evah! What a swell party this is!

He: Have you heard that Mrs. Cass
Had three beers and then ate the glass?
She: Well, did you evah! What a swell party this is.
He: Have you heard that Captain Craig
Breeds termites in his wooden leg?

Ethel Merman, Bert Lahr in DuBARRY WAS A LADY (1939)

She: Well, did you evah! What a swell party this is.
It's fun, it's fresh.
It's post depresh.
It's Shangrilah.
It's Harper's Bazaar!
What clothes, quel chic,
What pearls, they're the peak!
What glamour, what cheer!
He: This will simply slay you dear,
Kitty isn't paying calls,
She slipped over Niagara Falls.
She: Well, did you evah! What a swell party this is.
He: Have you heard that Mayor Hague
Just came down with bubonic plague?
She: Well, did you evah! What a swell party this is.

Copyright © 1940 by Chappell & Co., Inc.
Copyright Renewed

LET'S BE BUDDIES

Copyright © 1940 by Chappell & Co., Inc.
Copyright Renewed

Refrain (broad and with warmth)
B♭7 E♭ G7 C7 B♭ C7
Hattie: What say, let's be bud - dies, What
p-mf
F7 Gm 7+ F7 Fm7(♭5) E♭ F7
say, let's be pals, What
B♭7 E♮ dim. B♭7 E♭
say, let's be bud - dies, And keep up each
E♮ dim. Fm7 B♭7 E♭ G7
oth - er's mor - ales, I may nev - er
p

C7 B♭ C7 Fm G♯dim. C7
shout it, But ma - ny's the time, I'm
A♭ Gm7 C7 F7 F♯dim.
blue, What say, how's a -
espr. e crescendo
mf più espr.
E♭ poco rit. C7 Fm7 B♭7
bout it, Can't I be a bud - dy to
poco rit.
rallent.
1. E♭ F7 B♭7
2. E♭ F9 E♭
you? What you?
mf a tempo
p

I'VE STILL GOT MY HEALTH

"Panama Hattie"

Words and Music by
COLE PORTER

Copyright © 1940 by Chappell & Co., Inc.
Copyright Renewed

G♭ A♭7 D♭7 G♭ E♭m A♭m7
all the same, I'm in the pink, My con-sti-tu - tion's made of zinc, And you
G♭ C7+ E♭7 A♭m7 B♮7 B♭7
nev - er have to give this goil, Oil, Cas - tor.
mf
Refrain (brightly)
E♭ B♭7 E♭
I'm al - ways a flop at a top notch af -
p - mf
B♭7 E♭ C7 Fm7 B♭7 E♭ B♭7 sus. 4
fair, I've still got my health so what do I care!

Eb
Fm7
Bb7
Eb
Bb7
Eb
My best ring, a - las is a glass sol - i -
Bb7
Eb
C7
Fm7
Bb7
taire, I've still got my health so what do I
Eb
Bb7 sus. 4
F#dim.
Gm
D7
Gm
care! By fash - ion and
mp poco a
Cm7
C#dim.
Cm6
Gm
F7
fopp' - ry I'm nev - er dis - cussed, At -
poco crescendo
mf

B♭m E♭m7 C7 F7 B♭7
tend - ing the op' - ry, My box would be a bust!
B♭7 E♭ B♭7 E♭
I nev - er shall have that Park Av - e - nue
p
B♭7 E♭ C7 Fm7 B♭7
air, Well, I've still got my health so what do I
mf
1. E♭ Fm7 A♭ G7 B♭7
care! I
mf
2. E♭ A♭ E♭
care!
sf

I'VE STILL GOT MY HEALTH

REFRAIN 1
I'm always a flop at a top-notch affair,
But I've still got my health, so what do II care!
My best ring, alas, is a glass solitaire,
But I've still got my health, so what do I care!
By fashion and fopp'ry
I'm never discussed,
Attending the op'ry,
My box would be a bust!
When I give a tea, Lucius Beebe ain't there,
Well, I've still got my health, so what do I care!

VERSE 2
In spite of my Lux Movie skin
And Brewster body,
I've never joined the harem in
Scheherazade,
But, if so far, I've been a bust,
I'm stronger than the Bankers Trust
And you never have to give *this* one
Hunyadi.

REFRAIN 2
No rich Vanderbilt gives me gilt underwear,
But I've still got my health, so what do I care!
I've never been dined by refined L. B. Mayer,
But I've still got my health, so what do I care!
When Barrymore, he played
With his wife of yore,
The lead Missus B played,
But I played Barrymore,
She chased me a block for a lock of my hair,
Well, I've still got my health, so what do I care!

REFRAIN 3
I haven't the face of Her Grace, Ina Claire,
But I've still got my health, so what do I care!
I can't count my ribs, like His Nibs, Fred Astaire,
But I've still got my health, so what do I care!
Once I helped Jock Whitney
And as my reward,
I asked for a Jitney—
In other words, a Ford,
What I got from Jock was a sock, you know where,
Well, I've still got my health, so what do I care!

REFRAIN 4
When I'm in New York, I'm the Stork Club's despair,
But I've still got my health, so what do I care!
No radio chain wants my brain on the air,
But I've still got my health, so what do I care!
At school I was noted
For my lack of speed,
In fact I was voted
"Least likely to succeed,"
My wisecracks, I'm told are like old Camembert,
Well, I've still got my health, so what do I care!

VERSE 3
When Broadway first reviewed this wench,
The Press was catty,
They all agreed I'd even stench
In Cincinnati.
But, if I laid an awful egg,
I'm still as hot as Mayor Hague,
So in case you want to start a fire,
Wire Hattie.

REFRAIN 5
The hip that I shake doesn't make people stare,
But I've still got my health, so what do I care!
The sight of my props never stops thoroughfare,
But I've still got my health, so what do I care!
I knew I was slipping
At Minsky's one dawn,
When I started stripping,
They hollered "Put it on!"
Just once Billy Rose let me pose in the bare,
Well, I've still got my vitamins A, B, C, D,
E, F, G, H,
I
Still have my
Health.

Copyright © 1940 by Chappell & Co., Inc.
Copyright Renewed

Joan Carroll and Ethel Merman perform LET'S BE BUDDIES in PANAMA HATTIE (1940)

MAKE IT ANOTHER OLD FASHIONED, PLEASE

"Panama Hattie"

Words and Music by
COLE PORTER

Copyright © 1940 by Chappell & Co., Inc.
Copyright Renewed

Cm
G7
Cm
F♯7
B♭
F7
feel so much slick - er, Well, that is, most_ of the
B♭sus. 4
B♭
D♭
E♭7
B♭m
A♭
time, _ But there are mo - ments, soon - er or lat - er, when it's
Fm7
Guitar tacet
A♭
F7
G
tough, I got_ to say, not to say: "Wait - er! _
ten.
ten.
Em
G7
Subito Slow Rhumba tempo
Em
G7
f
mf

C
Refrain (with much expression)
G7
C
Make it an - oth - er Old Fash - ioned, please,
p-mf
G7 sus. 4
G7
C
C♯dim.
G7
Make it an - oth - er doub - le Old Fash - ioned
C
C7
F
B♭
F
please,
Make it for one who's due To
mf
C
Gm(add6)
A7 sus. 4
A7
Dm
A7
join the dis - il - lus - ioned crew,
Make it for one of love's

Dm
G7
F
B♭m
G7
C
new, ref - u - gees, Once high in my cas - tle,
espr.
p
G7
C
G7 sus. 4
G7
C7
I reigned su - preme, And Oh! what a cas - tle
poco - a - poco
C7
Am7
Dm
E7
built on a heav - en - ly dream, Then
cresc.
D7
E7
A7
Dm
Dm7
quick as a light - ning flash, That cas - tle be - gan to crash, So
mf

C
D7
G7
1. C
G7
make it an-oth-er Old Fash - ioned please!
p
mf
To Coda
2. C
Final ending
C6
C
Coda
G7
please!
please!
Leave out the
mf
p
C
G7
C
G7
cher-ry
Leave out the o-range!
Leave out the
Gm7
A7
D7
Dm7
Dm7(♭5)
C
bit-ters!
Just make it a straight rye!
mf
espr.
f molto cresc.
sf

SO NEAR AND YET SO FAR

You'll Never Get Rich

Words and Music by
COLE PORTER

Copyright © 1941 by Chappell & Co., Inc.
Copyright Renewed

C A7 Dm7 G7 C Dm7 G7
(more rhythmically)
time I start To o-pen my heart you van-ish We might
mf mf p
C C7
(soft again)
C G7
find some isle where lo-tus-es smile And our
Am7 A7 Dm A7 Dm G
(rhythmically
time be-guile go-ing na-tive But how
mf
C C7+ F6 G7 C
again)
Guitar tacet
can we go un-less you are co-op-er-a-tive?

Refrain (Tempo of Slow Rhumba)
B♭7
E♭
My dear, I've a feel-ing you are
mf
p-f
So near and yet so far,
Fm7
You ap-pear like a ra-di-ant star,
E♭7
First so near, then a-gain, so far.
cresc.

Eb7
Ab
Fm7
Bb7
Eb
I just start get-ting you keen on clinch-es ga - lore with me,
più espressivo
Bbm6
C7
When Fate steps in on the scene and mops up the
f
Fm7
Bb7
Bb7+
Eb
Bb7
floor with me.
No won - der
I'm a bit un-der
mf
p
Bbm6
C7
F7(9)
Bb7
Bb+
par.
For you're so near
and yet so
mf

Eb
Fm7
Bb7
Eb
far.
My con - di - tion is on - ly so so,
mf
Fm7
Bb7
Bbm
C7
'Cause when ev - er I feel you're close, oh you turn out to be
F7(9)
Bb7
1. Eb
Bb7+
oh so far.
My
mf
2. Eb
Eb7
Eb
far.
p
morendo
pp
pp

Rita Hayworth, Fred Astaire in the film musical YOU'LL NEVER GET RICH (1941)

EV'RYTHING I LOVE

"Let's Face It"

Copyright © 1941 by Chappell & Co., Inc.
Copyright Renewed

D♭7
G♭
B♭
I happen to know it, But any-way, Here's a
cresc.
mf
G♭7
C7
F7
B♭7
roun-de-lay, That I wrote last night a-bout you.
dim.
rit.
E♭
E♭+
A♭maj. 7
Refrain (slowly, with expression)
You are to me ev-'ry-
p - mf
a tempo
Fm
B♭7
B♭+
E♭
thing, My life to be, ev-'ry-

E♭6
E♭+
A♭
thing, When in my sleep you ap -
cresc.
mf
C7
D♭7
E♭7 E♮dim. D♭7
B♭
pear, Fair skies of deep blue ap -
espr.
B♭7
E♭
E♭+
A♭maj. 7
pear, Each time our lips touch a -
Fm
B♭7
D7
G
gain, I yearn for you oh so much a -
cresc.

Cm
Db6
Edim.
gain, You are my fav'-rite star,_ My
mf più espressivo
Ab
C7
F7
Eb
C7
ha - ven in heav - en a - bove, You are
p
1. Fm
Bb7
Eb
Cm
Abmaj. 7 F9
Bb7+
ev - 'ry - thing I love.
2. Fm7
Bb7
Eb
Bb9+
Eb6
ev - 'ry - thing I love.
p
8

FARMING

"Let's Face It"

Words and Music by
COLE PORTER

Copyright © 1941 by Chappell & Co., Inc.
Copyright Renewed

C7
F7
B♭7
E♭7
A-cres of al-fal-fa, fields of clo-ver Sud-den-ly en-chant our top "Who's who,"
mp
A♭
E♭7
A♭7
G7
G♭7
F7
E♭7
A♭
G7
So the mo-ment all this row is o-ver What say if we go hay-seed too, For
p
Cm
Refrain (faster and brigiter)
B♭6
G7
Cm
Farm - ing, that's the fash - ion, Farm - ing,
p-f
D7
G7
Cm
E♭
A♭6
that's the pas - sion of our great ce - leb - ri - ties of to - day,

E♭ B♭7 E♭ B♭7 E♮dim. B♭7
Fan - nie Hurst is haul - in' logs, —
E♭ B♭7 E♭ Cm6
Fan - nie Brice is call - in' hogs, — Gar - Bo - peep has led
cresc.
Cm F♯dim. G D7 G7 Cm
— her sheep all a - stray, — Hoe - ing —
mf
mp
B♭6 G7 Cm D7 G7
new po - ta - toes Throw - ing — old to - ma toes

C7
Fm
Fm6
G7
Makes 'em feel more glam - our - ous and more gay, They
Cm
C7
F7
tell me cows who are feel - ing milk - y All give cream when they're
mf
Ab
Bb7
Eb
F#dim.
Fm7(sus. 4)
Fm7
Bb7
milked by Will - kie, Farm - ing is so charm - ing, they all
mf
1. Eb
G7
2. Eb
say.
say.
f
8

Jack Williams, Nanette Fabray, Danny Kaye, Sunnie O'Dea, and Benny Baker perform FARMING in LET'S FACE IT (1941)

REFRAIN 1

Farming, that's the fashion,
Farming, that the passion
Of our great celebrities of today.
Kit Cornell is shellin' peas,
Lady Mendl's climbin' trees,
Dear Mae West is at her best in the hay,
Stomping through the thickets,
Romping with the crickets,
Makes 'em feel more glamorous and more gay,
They tell me cows who are feeling milky
All give cream when they're milked by Willkie,
Farming is so charming, they all say.

REFRAIN 2

Farming, that's the fashion,
Farming, that's the passion
Of our great celebrities of today.
Monty Woolley, so I heard,
Has boll weevils in his beard,
Michael Strange has got the mange, will it stay?
Mussing up the clover,
Cussing when it's over,
Makes 'em feel more glamorous and more gay.
The natives think it's utterly utter
When Margie Hart starts churning her butter,
Farming is so charming, they all say.

REFRAIN 3

Farming, that's the fashion,
Farming, that's the passion
Of our great celebrities of today.
Fannie Hurst is haulin' logs,
Fannie Brice is feedin' hogs,
Garbo-Peep has led her sheep all astray,
Singing while they're rakin',
Bringing home the bacon,
Makes 'em feel more glamorous and more gay.
Miss Elsa Maxwell, so the folks tattle,
Got well-goosed while de-horning her cattle,
Farming is so charming, they all say.

REFRAIN 4

Farming that's the fashion,
Farming, that's the passion
Of our great celebrities of today.
Don't inquire of Georgie Raft
Why his cow has never calfed,
Georgia's bull is beautiful, but he's gay!
Seeing spring a-coming,
Being minus plumbing,
Makes 'em feel informal and dégagé.
When Cliff Odets found a new tomater
He ploughed under the Group Theaytre,
Farming is so charming, they all say.

REFRAIN 5

Farming, that's the fashion,
Farming, that's the passion,
Of our great celebrities of today.
Steinbeck's growing Grapes of Wrath,
Guy Lombardo, rumor hath,
Toots his horn and all the corn starts to sway,
Racing like the dickens,
Chasing after chickens,
Makes 'em feel more glamorous and more gay,
Liz Whitney has, on her bin of manure, a
Clip designed by the Duke of Verdura,
Farming is so charming, they all say.

(Among the discarded lines were the following:)

Farming, that's the fashion,
Farming, that's the passion
Of our great celebrities of today.
Digging in his fertile glen,
Goldwyn dug up Anna Sten,
Fred Astaire has raised a hare and its gray.
Clowning in their mittens,
Drowning extra kittens,
Makes 'em feel more glamorous and more gay.
Paul Whiteman, while he was puttin' up jelly,
Ate so much he recovered his belly,
Farming is so charming, they all say.

Farming, that's the fashion,
Farming, that's the passion,
Of our great celebrities of today
Missus Henry Morganthau
Looks so chic behind a plow,
Mrs. Hearst is at her worst on a dray.
Tearing after pôssum,
Wearing just a blossom,
Makes 'em feel more glamorous and more gay,
Why Orson Welles, that wonderful actor,
Has Del Rio driving a tractor.
Farming is so charming, they all say.

Farming, that's the fashion,
Farming, that's the passion,
Of our great celebrities of today.
Just to keep her roosters keen,
Dietrich that great movie queen,
Lifts her leg and lays an egg, what a lay.
Going after rabbits,
Knowing all their habits,
Makes 'em feel more glamorous and more gay.
So Harpo Marx, in a moment of folly,
Had his barn repainted by Dali.
Farming is so charming, they all say.

Farming, that's the fashion,
Farming, that's the passion,
Of our great celebrities of today.
Lynn Fontanne is brandin' steer,
Sophie Tucker, so I hear,
Rides en masse upon an ass, hip-hooray.
Hoeing new potatoes,
Throwing all tomatoes,
Makes 'em feel more glamorous and more gay.
So Clifton Webb has parked his Ma, Mabel,
"Way Down East" in a broken-down stable,
Farming is so charming, they all say.

Copyright © 1941 by
Chappell & Co., Inc. Copyright Renewed

LET'S NOT TALK ABOUT LOVE

REFRAIN 2

Let's talk about frogs, let's talk about toads,
Let's try to solve the riddle why chickens
cross roads,
Let's talk about games, let's talk about sports,
Let's have a big debate about ladies in shorts,
Let's question the synonymy of freedom
and autonomy,
Let's delve into astronomy, political economy,
Or if you're feeling biblical, the book
of Deuteronomy,
But let's not talk about love.
Let's ride the New Deal, like Senator Glass,
Let's telephone to Ickes and order more gas,
Let's curse the Old Guard and Hamilton Fish,
Forgive me, dear, if Fish is your favorite dish,
Let's heap some hot profanities on Hitler's
inhumanities,
Let's argue if insanity's the cause of
his inanities,
Let's weigh the Shubert Follies with The Ear-rl
Carroll Vanities,
But let's not talk about love.
Let's talk about drugs, let's talk about dope,
Let's try to picture Paramount minus Bob Hope,
Let's start a new dance, let's try a new step,
Or investigate the cause of Missus Roosevelt's pep,
Why not discus, my dee-arie,
The life of Wallace Bee-ery
Or bring a jeroboam on
And write a drunken poem on
Astrology, mythology,
Geology, philology,
Pathology, psychology,
Electro-physiology,
Spermology, phrenology,
I owe you an apology
But let's not talk about love.

REFRAIN 3

Let's speak of Lamarr, the Hedy so fair,
Why does she let Joan Bennett wear all
her old hair?
If you know Garbo, then tell me this news,
Is it a fact the Navy's launched all
her old shoes?
Let's check on the veracity of Barrymore's
bibacity
And why his drink capacity should get so
much publacity,
Let's even have a huddle over Ha'vard
Univassity,
But let's not talk about love.
Let's wish him good luck, let's wish him
more pow'r,
That Fiorella fella, my favorite flow'r,
Let's get some champagne from over
the seas,
And drink to Sammy Goldwyn,
Include me out please.
Let's write a tune that's playable,
a ditty swing-and-swayable
Or say whatever's sayable, about the
Tow'r of Ba-abel,
Let's cheer for the career of itty-bitty
Betty Gra-abel,
But let's not talk about love.
In case you play cards, I've got some
right here
So how about a game o' gin-rummy, my dear?
Or if you feel warm and bathin's your whim,
Let's get in the all-together and
enjoy a short swim,
No honey, Ah suspect you all
Of bein' intellectual
And so, instead of gushin' on,
Let's have a big discussion on
Timidity, stupidity, solidity, frigidity,
Avidity, turbidity, Manhattan, and viscidity,
Fatality, morality, legality, finality,
Neutrality, reality, or Southern hospitality,
Pomposity, verbosity,
You're losing your velocity
But let's not talk about love.

Copyright © 1941 by Chappell & Co., Inc.
Copyright Renewed

LET'S NOT TALK ABOUT LOVE

"Let's Face It"

Words and Music by
COLE PORTER

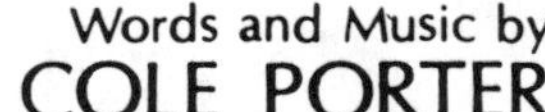

Tempo di Barcarolle
VOICE
Piano
mf
SHE
Re - lax for one mo-ment, my Jer - ry, Come out of your dark mon - as - te - ry While
Ve - nus is beam-ing a - bove, Dar - ling, let's talk a - bout love.
HE
My
Valse tempo
bud - dies all tell me se - lec - tees Are ex - pect - ed by
C
Dm7
G7
G7+
Fm7
C7

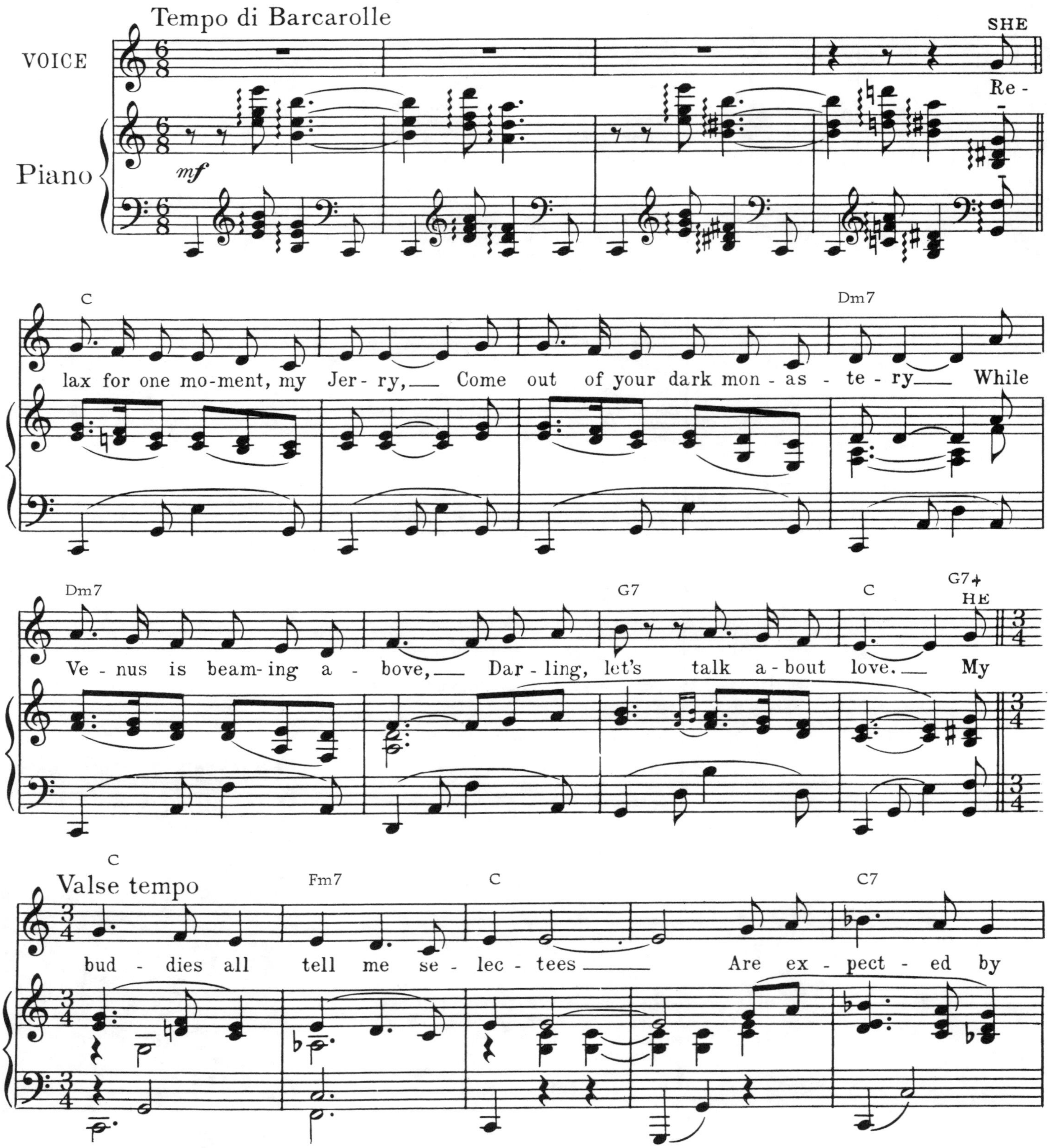

Copyright © 1941 by Chappell & Co., Inc.
Copyright Renewed

C7 Am D7 F♯dim.
la - dies to neck - tease, I could talk a - bout love and why
C A7 Dm7 G7
not? But be - lieve me, it would - n't be so hot, So let's
poco rit.
Refrain
Lightly and rhythmically
C F6 C Fm6 C G7
talk a - bout frogs, Let's talk a - bout toads, Let's try to solve the rid-dle why
p
F♯dim. C7 F B♭ F B♭m6
chick-ens cross roads, Let's talk a - bout games, Let's talk a - bout sports, Let's

F C7 G♯dim. F Fm6 C Cm F♯dim.
have a big de - bate a - bout la - dies in shorts, Let's check on the ve - ra - ci - ty of
G7 C Cm F♯dim. G7
Bar-ry-more's bi-ba-ci-ty And why his drink ca-pa-ci-ty should get so much pub-la-ci-ty, Let's
C A Dm7 C G7
e - ven have a hud - dle o - ver Ha'- vard U - ni - va - si - ty, But let's not talk a - bout
C F♯dim. G7 C F C Fm6 C G7
love Let's wish him good luck, Let's wish him more pow'r That Fi - o - rel - la fel - la, my
mf
p

F♯dim. C7 F B♭6 F B♭m6
fav - or - ite flow'r Let's curse the Old Guard and Ham - il - ton Fish, For -
F C7 G♯dim. F Fm6 C Cm F♯dim.
give me, dear if Fish is your fav - or - ite dish, Let's write a tune that's play - a - ble, a
G7 C Cm F♯dim. G7
dit - ty swing-and-sway - a - ble, Or say what ev - er's say - a - ble a - bout the Tow'r of Ba - a - bel, Let's
C A Dm7 C G7
cheer for the ca - reer of it - ty - bit - ty Bet - ty Gra - a - ble, But let's not talk a - bout

C Dm7 C G7 B♭m6 F G7 B♭m6
love. Let's talk a - bout drugs, Let's talk a-bout dope, Let's try to pic-ture Par-a-mount
mf
mp
poco a poco cresc.
F D7 Cm6 G E7
mi - nus Bob Hope, Let's start a new dance, Let's try a new step, Or in -
Cm6 G E♭7 D7 G7 faster C Cm F♯dim.
ves - ti - gate the cause of Mis-sus Roos - e - velt's pep, Why not dis-cuss, my dee - a - rie, The
mf
G7 C Cm F♯dim. G7
life of Wal - lace Bee-a - ry, Or bring a jer - o - bo-am on And write a drunk-en po-em on Ti -

faster and faster
C G7 C G7 C G7
mid - i - ty, stu-pid - i - ty, sol - id - i - ty, fri-gid - i - ty, a - vid - i - ty, tur-bid - i - ty, Man-
C G7 C G7 C G7
hat-tan and vi-cid - i - ty, Fa-tal - i - ty, mo-ral - i - ty, le - gal - i - ty, fi-nal - i - ty, Neu-
C G7 C G7 C
tral - i - ty, re-al - i - ty or south-ern hos-pi-tal - i - ty, Pom - pos - i - ty, ver-bos - i - ty, I'm
F A♭7 C C+ D7 G7 1. C Em G7 2. C
los-ing my ve-loc - i - ty, But let's not talk a - bout love. Let's love.
sf

I HATE YOU, DARLING

"Let's Face It"

Words and Music by
COLE PORTER

Copyright © 1941 by Chappell & Co., Inc.
Copyright Renewed

B♭m6
I should be clev - er
C7
B♭m6
Fm
Fm7
Fm
and say "good-bye," Good-bye, for - ev - er, my but-ter-fly.
Am9
A♭m6
B♭7
Fm
D♭7
B♭7
But why be clev - er, When dar-ling I need The
E♭
Fm7
B♭7
E♭
A♭
E♭
joy you bring more than an - y - thing I know. I'm in the

D♭6
E♭7
Cm7
A♭dim.
B♭m7
depths of Inferno When you're far away
mp
A♭6
passionately
F7
from me, dear. But when our sweet nights re-
mf
E♮dim.
Cm7
suddenly hot
F7
turn, Oh, my hab-i-tat, Is the strat-o-sphere.
f
B♭
B♭7
B♭m6
With tender expression, as before
Still I hate you dar-ling
mp

C7
Bbm6
Fm
Fm7
It's true my pet
I hate you dar - ling
Fm
Am9
Abm6
Cm7
Bbm9
C7
But don't for - get
I hate you dar - ling
cresc.
F7
Abm6
Eb
Ab6
And yet I love you so.
espr.
f marcato
1. Eb
Fm7
Bb7
2. Eb
I
mf
f

YOU'D BE SO NICE TO COME HOME TO

"Something To Shout About"

Words and Music by
COLE PORTER

Copyright © 1942 by Chappell & Co., Inc.
Copyright Renewed

B♭7 E♭ B♭ E♭7 A♭
not that you're rar - er Than as - par - a - gus out of sea - son, No, my
B♮ E♭ Cm6 E♭dim. E♭ Fdim. D7 G
dar - ling, this is the reas - on Why you've got to be mine:
rit. p mf
F E7 Am Dm6 E7 Am E7
Refrain (rather slow with feeling)
ten. ten.
You'd be so nice to come home to,
p - mf a tempo
Am C7 F C+
You'd be so nice by the fire,

F
Am
Dm7
B7(♭5)
E7
While the breeze, on high, sang a
D dim.
Am
G7
Am6
F7
B7
lull - a - by, You'd be all that I could de -
mf
E
B7
E
D
E7
Am
Dm6
E7
sire, Un - der stars, chilled by the
p
Am
E7
Am
C7
win - ter, Un - der an Aug - ust moon,
3
cresc.

F
C+
F
A
Dm
Burn - ing a - bove,
You'd be
C dim.
C
F
Fm6
so nice, You'd be par - a - dise to come
cresc.
mf espr.
1. C
Ab7
D7
G7
C
F
E7
home to and love. You'd be
f
mf
2. C
Ab7
D7
G7
C
home to and love.
f espr.
p

COULD IT BE YOU

"Something For The Boys"

Words and Music by
COLE PORTER

Copyright © 1942 by Chappell & Co., Inc.
Copyright Renewed

Refrain, (Slowly, with expression)
B♭ F9 B♭ G♭m Fm B♭7 E♭
Could it be you, The one I'm fat - ed for? Could it be
B♭9 E♭ C7 F
you, The love I've wait - ed for? For lo, since
Edim. F7 G9 G♭7 F7 A dim. Gm Gm7
you came a - long, And kin-dled the song in my heart, Why both - er pre -
C7 F7 C9 Cm7 F7 B♭
tend - ing? The song is un - end - ing. Are you the
p
mf
cresc.
rit.

F9
B♭
G♭m
Fm
B♭7
E♭
dream, I al - ways dream a - bout? Are we the
B♭9
E♭
C7
B♭
team I'm on the beam a - bout? Could be, these
mf espr.
D7
E♭
B♭
G7
E♭m
B♭
rev'-ries of mine, Are far too di - vine to come true, Or could it
C9
Cm7
F7
1. B♭
Cm7
F7
2. B♭
be re - al - ly you? you?
rit.
mp a tempo
mf
p

I LOVE YOU

"Mexican Hayride"

Words and Music by
COLE PORTER

Copyright © 1943 by Chappell & Co., Inc.
Copyright Renewed

F
un pochettino più mosso
B♭m
F6
Fmaj. 7
F7
las, just an am - a - teur am I ______ And so I'll
B♭
E♭m
B♭+
Gm
D7
not be sur - prised, my dear ______ If you
mf
G7
F dim.
F
calmato
smile and po - lite - ly pass it by ______ When this, my
più mosso
pp
G7
Gm7
C7
F
(four beats)
first love song, you hear ______
rit
a tempo

Refrain (in warm movement)
B♭m6
C7
Fdim.
F
"I love you" Hums the A - pril breeze
p-mf
Gm7
C7
3
"I love you" ech - o the
F
D7
B♭m6
hills. "I love you"
C7
Fdim.
F
the gold - en dawn a - grees As once

A
E7
A7
more she sees daf - fo - dils.
poco a poco cresc.
Gm7
appassionato
C7
It's spring a - gain And birds on the
f
F
Cm6
wing a - gain start to sing a - gain
D7
Cm
D7
G7
C7
The old mel - o - die "I

B♭m6
Tempo I
C7
Fdim.
F
F7
D7
love you" That's the song of songs, And it
G7
C7
1. F
Fdim.
C7(sus. 4)
C7
all be-longs to you and me. I
mf
2. F
B♭
F
B♭m
me And it all be - longs to you and
p
delicato
poco sostenuto
F
me.
p
pp

EV'RY TIME WE SAY GOODBYE

"Seven Lively Arts"

Words and Music by
COLE PORTER

Copyright © 1944 by Chappell & Co., Inc.
Copyright Renewed

Refrain, Very slowly and pensively (four beats)
Eb Cm Eb Cm Eb Cm Fm7 Bb7
Ev - 'ry time we say good - bye I die a lit-tle,
p-mf
Eb Bb7 Gb Bb7 Eb Eb7
Ev - 'ry time we say good - bye I won-der
Abm Eb Ebdim. Abm6 Bb7
why a lit - tle, Why the gods a - bove me Who
mf
Bbm Eb7 Ab Abm
must be in the know Think so lit-tle

Eb- Eb Ebdim. Ebm Bb7 Abm Bb7
of me They al - low you to go
3
p
mf
Eb Cm Eb Cm Eb Cm
When you're near there's such an air of
p
Fm7 Bb7 Eb Bb7 Gb Bb7
Spring a - bout it, I can hear a lark some -
Eb Eb7 Ab Abm Eb Ebdim.
where be - gin to sing a - bout it, There's no love song
f espressivo

A♭m6 B♭7 E♭7 A♭ A♭m
fin - er, But how strange the change from ma - jor to mi - nor
subito p
E♭ C7 1 F7 A♭ B♭7 E♭ E♭dim. B♭7
Ev - 'ry time we say good - bye.
p
f
2. F7 Fm7 B♭7 Cm E♭dim. B♭7 B♭m Cm7
we say good - bye. Ev-'ry sin-gle time we
espr.
mf
F7 B♭7 E♭ Cm E♭ Cm E♭ Cm E♭
say good - bye.
f rit.
R.H.
mf
morendo
pp

Original sheet music cover designs

1942

1944

1944

1943

USE YOUR IMAGINATION

"Out Of This World"

Words and Music by
COLE PORTER

Copyright © 1950 by Cole Porter
Chappell & Co., Inc., publisher and owner of publication and allied rights throughout the world

A♭
C7
Fm
take this mot-to for your theme
And
B♭7
E♭
A♭
A♭m
E♭
C dim.
soon ev-'ry night will be crowd-ed with de-light
And
E♭
F7
B♭7
Fm7
B♭7
ev-'ry day will be a dream,
mf
dim
E♭
Cm6
B♭7
E♭
E♭7
Use your i-ma-gi-na-tion,
You'll
p
R.H.
8

A♭
C7
Fm
see such won-ders if you do, A -
B♭7
E♭
A♭
A♭m
E♭
C dim.
round you there lies pure en - chant-ment in dis - guise And
E♭
Fm
B♭7
E♭
end - less joys you nev-er knew, Be -
(♭)
A♭m
E♭
Fm7
B♭7
E♭
hind ev - 'ry cloud there's a so love - ly star, Be -
mf

Cm D7 Gm Cm7 F7 B♭7
hind ev - 'ry star there's a love - li - er one by far So
ten.
cresc.
f poco rit.
E♭ Cm6 B♭7 E♭ E♭7
use your i - ma - gi - na - tion, Just
p a tempo
R.H.
A♭ C7 Fm
take this mot - to for your theme And
B♭7 E♭ A♭ A♭m E♭ F7
soon you will dance on the road to sweet ro - mance And
rit.
mf

E♭
A♭
B♭7
1. E♭
E♭dim. E♭
F7
B♭7
ev - 'ry day will be a dream.
p poco rit.
a tempo
2. Cm
A♭
E♭
Cm
A♭
dream
And ev - 'ry
p slower
F9
B♭7
day will be a per - - fect
mf
molto cresc.
f
rall.
E♭
dream.
p begin faster
slower
pp
R.H.
Ped.
pp

FROM THIS MOMENT ON

"Out Of This World"

Words and Music by
COLE PORTER

Copyright © 1950 by Cole Porter
Chappell & Co., Inc., publisher and owner of publication and allied rights throughout the world

F
Gm7
C7
F
Now that we're side by side, the future looks so
p dolce
Dm7
G
Dm
C
Dm7
G7
gay, Now we are al - i - bi ed when we
C
Suddenly lively
Gm6
Am
C7
say:
mf
accel. e cresc.
f
Fm
Refrain (lively, but not rushed)
Gm7
C7
From this mo - ment on,
mf

B♭m6
Fm
E♭m
A♭7
you for me, dear,
D♭
D♭m
on - ly two for tea, dear,
A♭
A♭dim.
C7
from this mo - ment on.
Fm
Gm7
C7
From this hap - py day,
mf
f

B♭m6
Fm
E♭m7
A♭7
no more blue songs,
D♭
D♭m
on - ly whoop - dee - doo songs,
A♭
E♭7
A♭7
from this mo - ment on.
For you've
mf
f
D♭
D♭m
got the love I need so much,

A♭
E♭m7
F7
Got the skin I love to touch,
E♭
B♭7
Got the arms to hold me tight,
mf
cresc.
E♭
Got the sweet lips to kiss me good-night,
p subito
Fm
Gm7
C7
From this moment on,
mf

B♭m6 Fm E♭m7 A♭7
you and I, babe,
D♭ D♭m6 A♭
we'll be rid - in' high, babe, Ev - 'ry
cresc.
f
A♭dim A♭ A♭7 F7 B♭7 D♭ E♭7
care is gone from this mo - ment
1. A♭ C7
on.
dim.
2. A♭
on.
sf

I AM LOVED

"Out Of This World"

Words and Music by
COLE PORTER

Copyright © 1950 by Cole Porter
Chappell & Co., Inc., publisher and owner of publication and allied rights throughout the world

oh, to - day, to - day is a gay day, You
f espressivo
dim.
poco rit.
p
Dm
Em
Dm7
G7
ask me, dar - ling, why? And I an - swer:
più rit.
C
Refrain (Slow Beguine tempo, with great expression)
I am loved, I am loved
mp
Gm7
C7
by the one I love in ev - 'ry

F
Dm7
way,
I
am
loved,
Cdim.
C
D7
D7(♭5)
ab - so - lute - ly
loved,
What
a
mf
subito p
C
Dm
C
won - der - ful
thing
to
be
a - ble
to
say.
I'm
a - dored,
I'm
a -
mf

dored by the one who
Gm7 C7 F
first led my heart a - stray,
I'm a -
Dm7 C♯dim. C
dored, ab - so - lute - ly a - dored,
mf
Dm
D7 D7(♭5) C Dm
What a won - der - ful thing to be a - ble to
subito p

C
say.
So ring out the bells
molto cresc.
f
Db7
molto espr.
Gb
and let the trum-pets blow
And
f
D7
beat on the drums
for now I know I
ff più espr.
Dm7
dim. e rit.
G7
know I am loved,
I am
mp
C
a tempo
Cnaj. 7
cresc.

Am6
D9
D7(♭5)
C
loved,
What a won-der-ful thing,
p
Dm
C
F
What a glor-i-ous thing,
What a
C
Dm
1. C
beau-ti-ful thing
to be a-ble to say.
poco rit.
più rit.
a tempo
D7
G7
2. C
I am say.
mp
a tempo
pp
pp

WHERE, OH WHERE

"Out Of This World"

Words and Music by
COLE PORTER

Copyright © 1950 by Cole Porter
Chappell & Co., Inc., publisher and owner of publication and allied rights throughout the world

G
Fm7
B♭7
Gm7
deal? For e - ven though, when I'm a - bed,
poco rit.
E♭
B♭7
E♭
I dream he holds me tight, A -
poco accel.
G7(♭9)
G7+5
G7
Cm
Fm
Cm
wake, I nev - er light On the man I plan,
poco rit.
più rit.
G7
G7+
C
F
G7
one day, to wed.
mf subito in tempo
cresc.
f rit.

Refrain (Lilting and graceful Waltz tempo)
C Dm7 G7 C C dim. Dm7
Where, oh where is that com - bi - na - tion so rare,
mf
G7 C G Am7 G C A7
A cute knight in ar - mor, com - plete - ly a charm - er, who'd still be a mil - lion -
mp
D7 G7 C Dm7 G7
aire? Where, oh where is that
mf
C C dim. Dm7 G7 C G Am7
com - bi - na - tion so rare, A youth who is a - ble to wrap me in
mp

G C Am7 B+ B Em
sa - ble, who'd still be a love af - fair? I could ac - cept a
mp
F♯7 B7 Em G
cot - tage small, by a roar - ing wa - ter - fall, Yet I'd much pre -
p
F♯ Dm7 G7
fer a cas - tle cool, by a mar - ble swim - ming pool, But
poco rit.
C Dm7 G7 C C dim. Dm7
where, oh where is that com - bi - na - tion so rare,
mf a tempo

G7
C
G
Am7
G
C
G7
— A high - ly ad - miss - i - ble, kiss - a - ble boy to fill me with, prac - tic - 'lly
mp
cresc.
C
C7+
F
A dim.
C
A7
kill me with joy who'd still be a mil - lion - aire? Tell me
f
dim. e rit.
mf
F
Dm7
G7
1. C
where, oh where, oh where?
a tempo
p più rit.
a tempo
Dm7
G7
2. C
where?
a tempo
mf

Playbill for OUT OF THIS WORLD which opened Dec. 21, 1950 starring Charlotte Greenwood

Original sheet music cover for OUT OF THIS WORLD

YOU DON'T REMIND ME

SAINT SUBBER & LEMUEL AYERS
PRESENT COLE PORTER'S NEW MUSICAL PLAY

"OUT OF THIS WORLD"

LYRICS & MUSIC BY COLE PORTER
BOOK BY DWIGHT TAYLOR & REGINALD LAWRENCE
CHOREOGRAPHY BY HANYA HOLM
SETTINGS & COSTUMES DESIGNED BY LEMUEL AYERS
ENTIRE PRODUCTION STAGED BY AGNES DE MILLE

I Am Loved
Use Your Imagination
From This Moment On
You Don't Remind Me
Hark To The Song Of The Night
Where, Oh Where
Nobody's Chasing Me
Cherry Pies Ought To Be You
No Lover
Climb Up The Mountain

BUXTON HILL MUSIC CORPORATION
RKO BUILDING • Rockefeller Center • NEW YORK
Sole Selling Agent
CHAPPELL & CO., INC.

YOU DON'T REMIND ME

"Out Of This World"

Words and Music by
COLE PORTER

Copyright © 1950 by Cole Porter
Chappell & Co., Inc., publisher and owner of publication and allied rights throughout the world

C
Dm7
G7
C
blue - bird
starts
to
sing.
C
C+
Am
C7
B♭
C7
You
don't
re - mind
me
of
the
F
A7
A7+5
Dm
A
Dm
breeze
on
the
bay
or
of
A7
Em7
A7
Dm
Fm
stars
in
the
foun - tain
where
the

C
Dm7
G7
C
C7
sil - ver fish - es play. To the
F
moon - glow in Sep - tem - ber, You re -
mp poco a poco cresc.
veal no re - sem - blance, Of the
più espressivo
mp
G
first snow in No - vem - ber, you've not e - ven
poco a poco cresc.
più espressivo

F
G7
C
Em
— a sem - blance, No, you don't re -
p
Am
C7
B♭
C7
F
A7
mind me of the world a - round me or be -
molto cresc.
D7
C
Am7
hind me For so much does my love for you
mf
f
3
Dm7
C
C dim.
Dm7
blind me that, my dar - ling, you on - ly re - mind me

G7
Gm6
A7
D7
Fm
ten.
— of
you, ——
of
you, ——
of
ten.
dim
p
mf
dim.
ten.
1. C
Dm7
G7
you! ——
mp
f a tempo
mp
2. C
C+
Am
C+
you! ——
mf a tempo
C
p morendo
pp

IT'S ALL RIGHT WITH ME

"Can-Can"

Words and Music by
COLE PORTER

Copyright © 1953 by Cole Porter
Chappell & Co., Inc., owner of worldwide publication and allied rights

F9
F7
G
Fm6
G
F
G7
all right with me. It's the
dim.
R.H.
mp
Cm
F9
wrong song in the wrong style tho' your
Cm
Fm
smile is love - ly, it's the wrong smile, it's not
B♭
B♭9
B♭7
B♭m6
C9
{her / his} smile but such a love - ly smile that it's
mf
sf

F9 Fm7 B♭7 E♭
all right with me. You
dim.
mf
B♭m E♭9 C dim.
can't know how hap - py I am that we met, I'm
A♭m F dim. E♭ E♭maj. 7 E♭6
strange - ly at - tract - ed to you, There's
B♭m6 C7(♭9) F7
some - one I'm try - ing so hard to for - get, Don't

Fm6
you want to for - get some - one too?
G7 Cm6 G F G7
It's the
Cm
wrong game with the
F9
wrong chips, tho' your
Cm
lips are tempt - ing, they're the
Fm
wrong lips, They're not
B♭ B♭9
{her / his} lips,
B♭7
but they're such
B♭m6 C9
tempt - ing lips that if
mp
mf
sf

F9
F7
B♭9
Gm
D
Fm 7
B♭7
some night
you're
free,
dear, it's
dim.
E♭maj. 7
E♭7
E♭7+
A♭maj. 7
all
right,
it's
all
right
cresc.
A♭7
F9
Fm 7
with
me.
f
1. E♭
G7
2. E♭
It's the
mp
sf

I LOVE PARIS

"Can-Can"

Words and Music by
COLE PORTER

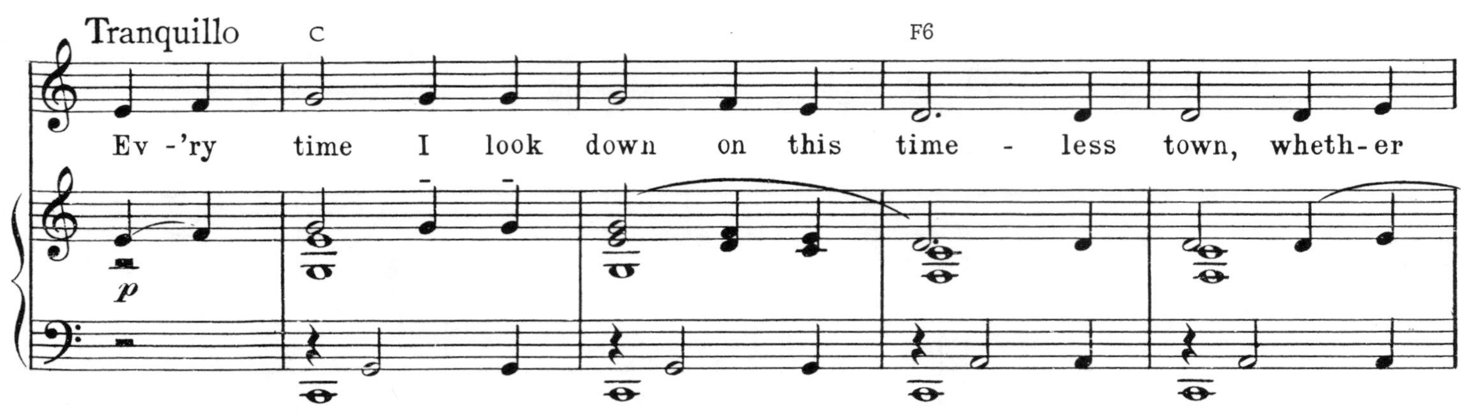

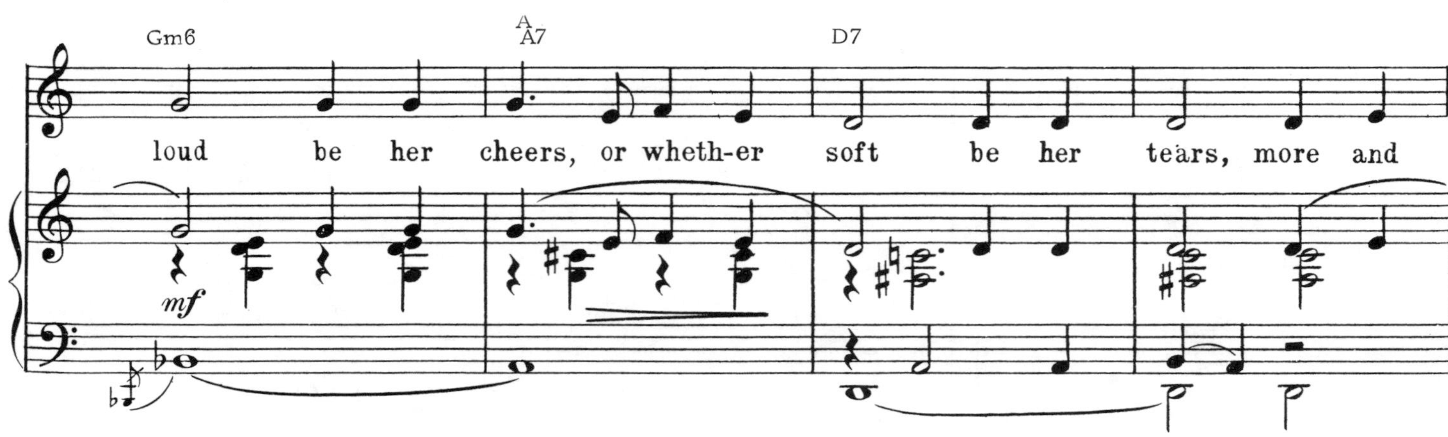

Copyright © 1953 by Cole Porter
Chappell & Co., Inc., owner or worldwide publication and allied rights

Fm6
G7(6)
F
G7(6)
G7
C
C dim.
G7(♭9)
more do I re - al - ize
poco rit.
Cm
Refrain (slow fox-trot tempo)
I love Par - is in the spring - time,
p legato
Cm
I love Par - is in the
G7
fall,
G7
I love

G7
Par - is in the win - ter, when it driz - zles,
G7
I love Par - is in the sum-mer, when it siz - zles,
Fm
G7
Cm
Sostenuto (jubilantly)
C
I love Par - is ev - 'ry mo - ment,
C
ev - 'ry mo - ment of the
C
Cdim.

G7
Dm7
G7
F
year,
I
love
C
F
C
Par - is,
why,
oh
why
do
I
love
Par - is?
1.
2.
G7
C
Cdim.
G7
A7(sus)
A7
Be-cause my
love
is
near.
Be-cause my
love
p
rit.
a tempo
mf
p cresc.
Dm7
G7(sus)
C
Be-cause my
love
is
near.
f
ff

ALLEZ-VOUS-EN, GO AWAY

"Can - Can"

Words and Music by
COLE PORTER

Copyright © 1953 by Cole Porter
Chappell & Co., Inc., owner of worldwide publication and allied rights

*Pronounce: Al-lay-voo-zon (French for Go away.)

C
C
G7
Al - lez-vous - en, go a - way,
Dm
Dm6
B♭
Al - lez-vous - en, al - lez-vous - en, Mam' - selle, M' - sieur,
Dm
Dm7
G7
C
C maj. 7
I have no time for you to - day,
mf
C6
C
C6
C +
Do be a dear, just dis - ap - pear Mam' - selle, M' - sieur,
p

C
C9
C+
F maj. 7
Bid me good - bye, do, do, do,
cresc.
F6
Dm7
C dim.
C
Al - lez - vous - en, please go a - way, {Mam' - selle, M' - sieur,
mf
mp
1.
C
G7
C
Gdim.
G7
or I may go a - way with you. Al - lez - vous -
p
rit.
mp a tempo
2.
C
G7
C
Dm
Cdim.
C
or I may go a - way with you.
mp
molto espr.
rit.
mf

C'EST MAGNIFIQUE

"Can-Can"

Copyright © 1953 by Cole Porter
Chappell & Co., Inc., owner of worldwide publication and allied rights

F
3
soon you will find, if you fol - low your heart, not your mind,
cresc.
B♭
F7
Gm
Love is wait - ing there a - gain, to take you up in the
f poco rit.
dim.
A7
D7
G
air a - gain.
mp a tempo
Refrain (Slow and easy)
G
G
When love comes in and takes you for a
mp

*Pronounced "say man-yee-fee-kuh"

G
G9
G7
loved one drifts a - way, oo la la-la,
It is so tra -
Cmaj. 7
C6
Am
C6
Cm6
gi - que.
But when, once more,
he
she
mf
espressivo
G
C
G
A7
D7(6)
whis-pers "Je t'a - dore" C'est mag-ni - fi
poco e poco rit. a tempo
1.
G
D7
que.
When
mp
2.
G
D7
G
que.
f
rit. e dim.

C'EST MAGNIFIQUE

VERSE 2

Aristide: When you began of love to speak,
I followed every word.
But when you called love magnifique,
I would have called it absurd
And when you said it was often tragique,
I would have said it was always comique.
So, mad'moiselle, be sweet to me
And kindly do not repeat to me.

Copyright © 1952 & 1953 by
Chappell & Co., Inc.

Shubert Theatre program cover for CAN-CAN (892 performances)

STEREOPHONIC SOUND

"Silk Stockings"

Words and Music by
COLE PORTER

Copyright © 1955 (unpub.) & 1958 by Cole Porter
Chappell & Co., Inc., owner of publication and allied rights throughout the world

A♭ D♭m A♭ B dim E♭7
Breath-tak-ing cin-e-ma-scope and Ste-re-o-phon-ic sound.
Breath-tak-ing cin-e-ma-scope and Ste-re-o-phon-ic sound.
E♭+ A♭ E♭+
If Zan-uck's la-test pic-ture were the
I late-ly did a pic-ture at the
mf
A♭ G A♭ G
good old-fash-ioned kind There'd be no-one in front to look at
bot-tom of the sea. I ras-sled with an oc-to-pus and
A♭ B9
Mar-i-lyn's be-hind. If you want to hear ap-plaud-ing hands re-
licked an an-cho-vee. But the pub-lic would-n't care if I had
cresc.

Pronounce "zound"

A♭ D♭ A♭
wide, You've got_ to have glo-ri-ous tech-ni-col-or, Breath-tak-ing
care Un-less_ she had glo-ri-ous tech-ni-col-or, Breath-tak-ing
D♭m 1. A♭ D♭m A♭
cin-e-ma-scope or Cin-e-ra-ma, Vis-ta-vi-sion, Su-per-scope or
cin-e-ma-scope or
mf sub.
D♭m A♭ C+ F7
**Tod-da-o and Ste-re-o-phon-ic sound,_ and
cresc.
ff
f
B♭9 E♭7(♭9) A♭ E♭7 E♭+
Ste-re-o-phon-ic sound._ You
ff
mf
**Pronounce "Tod-day-o"

2.
A♭
D♭m
A♭
D♭m
Cin - e - col - or or Warner - col - or or Pa - thé - col - or or East - man - col - or or
mf
A♭
D♭m
A♭
C7+
F7
Ko - da - col - or or an - y col - or and Ste - re - o - phon - ic sound
cresc.
E♮9
and Ste - re - o - phon - ic as an ex - tra
ff
f
A♭
B♭7(♭9)
A♭
ton - ic, Ste - re - o - phon - ic sound.
ff

AS ON THROUGH THE SEASONS WE SAIL

"Silk Stockings"

Words and Music by
COLE PORTER

Copyright © 1954 by Cole Porter
Chappell & Co., Inc., owner of publication and allied rights throughout the world

Bb
F7(bB)
F7
Bb
Bbdim.
Bb7
(She) I'll mar - ry you so wil - ling - ly.
(He) Ba - by,
poco rit.
Refrain (Moderate Fox-trot)
Eb
Abmaj. 7
Bb7
Eb
Abm
Bb7
I love you, oh I do, and this I'll prove to you, As
a tempo
mp
Eb
Gm
Fm
Eb
Gm
Fm
Bb7
Ab
Bb7
C7
on through the sea - sons we sail. Re -
mf
mp
Fm
Bbm7
C7
Fm
Abdim.
C7
mote from cra - zy crowds, we'll float a - bove the clouds, As

Fm7
Bb7
Eb
on through the sea - sons we sail.
mf
Bb7
Eb
Abmaj. 7
Bb7
When we are man and wife, I
mp
Eb
Abm
Bb7
Eb
swear to make our life A re - vo - lu - tion - ar - y
Eb9
Eb+
Ab
Abdim.
Ab
fair - y tale. How
mf

Fm
Bb7
Eb
Bb7
Bbm7
C7
hap - py we will be, once we are one, two or three, as
poco rit.
Fm
C7
1. Fm7
Bb7
Eb
Bbdim. Bb7
on through the sea - sons we sail.
I
a tempo
mf
mp
2. Fm7
G dim.
Bbm6
Fm
G dim.
Fm7
ten.
Bb7
sea - sons, As on through the sea - sons we
ten.
ten.
Eb
Ab
Eb
sail.
f
dim.

ALL OF YOU

"Silk Stockings"

Words and Music by
COLE PORTER

Copyright © 1954 by Cole Porter
Chappell & Co., Inc., owner of publication and allied rights throughout the world

Fm7
B♭7
G7+
G7
G dim.
C7
cer - tain love - ly lass, And it's
Fm
Fm7
B♭7
E dim.
B♭7
not a pass - ing fan - cy or a fan - cy pass.
f
Refrain - Slowly
A♭
E♭
I love the looks of you, the
mp
A♭m
A♭
E♭
lure of you, I'd love to make a

A♭m
E♭
E♭dim.
tour of you, The eyes, the arms, the
più espr.
B♭9
E♭
B♭m7
C7
C7(♭9)
C7+
mouth of you, The East, West, North and the
f
Fm
B♭7
A♭
E♭
South of you. I'd love to gain com -
mp
A♭m
A♭
E♭
plete con - trol of you, And han - dle

C7
Em
e - ven the heart and soul of you. So
cresc.
A♭
E♭ dim.
G7+
G7
love, at least, a small per-cent of me, do,
f marcato
B♭m6
C7
Fm
C7
Fm
B♭7
For I love all of
1. E♭
B dim.
B♭7
2. E♭
You. I love the You.
f
mf
f

Gretchen Wyler, Stanley Simmons *in* SILK STOCKINGS (1955)

TRUE LOVE

"High Society"

Words and Music by
COLE PORTER

Copyright © 1955 (unpub.) & 1956 by Chappell & Co., Inc.

Refrain (Rather slow)
G
C
G dim.
G
I give to you and you give to me
mp
a tempo
D7
C
G
True love, true love. So,
C
G dim.
G
on and on it will al - ways be
D7
G
Cm
True love, true love. For you and
cresc.

F7
B♭
G7
Cm
I have a guard - ian an - gel on high With
F7
B♭7
D7
G
noth - ing to do ___ But to give to
C
G dim.
G
D7
you and to give to me Love for - ev - er
poco rit.
1. G
C
D7
true. ___ I
2. G
true. ___
p

MIND IF I MAKE LOVE TO YOU

"High Society"

Words and Music by
COLE PORTER

Copyright © 1955 (unpub.) & 1956 by Chappell & Co., Inc.

A♭7
A♭maj. 7
B♭m7
E♭7
rare night for ro - manc - ing, Mind if
D♭m6
E♭7(♭9)
E♭7
A♭
A♭m6
E♭9
I make love to you? Since the
mf
A♭
B♭m7
dear day of our meet - ing I've want - ed to
3
E♭9
E♭9+5
A♭
tell you all I long to do Dawn is
3

A♭7
A♭maj. 7
B♭m7
E♭7
near - ing time is fleet - ing, Mind if
D♭m6
E♭7(♭9)
E♭7
E♭m6
F7
I make love to you? If you
B♭m
D♭m6
A♭
let me, I'll en - deav - or to per -
poco a poco cresc.
B♭7
E♭7 sus. A♭
E♭9
E♭9+5
suade you I'm your part - y for two And from
mf
mf

A♭
A♭7
D♭6
D♭m6
then on you will nev - er mind if
f
1. A♭
E♭9
E♭9sus. A♭
A♭
A♭m6
B♭m7
E♭9
I make love to you. In the
mf
2. A♭
E♭9
E♭9sus. A♭
I make love to
poco a poco dim.
A♭
you.
pp

YOU'RE SENSATIONAL

"High Society"

Words and Music by
COLE PORTER

Copyright © 1955 (unpub.) & 1956 by Chappell & Co., Inc.

Refrain (Fox-trot tempo, but not fast)
Fm7 Fm6 Fm7 Fm6 B♭7
He: I've no proof when peo - ple say you're
She: I've no proof when peo - ple say you're
mp
Fm7 B♭7 Fm7 B♭7 E♭ Gm E♭
more or less a - loof But you're sen
more or less a - loof But you're sen
Gm7 E♭ Fm7 B♭7
sa - tion - al. I don't care
sa - tion - al. I don't care
A♭ Fm7 Fm6 B♭7 Fm7 B♭7 Fm7 B♭7
if you are called "The Fair Miss Frig - id Air"
if you are known as Mis - ter Frig - id Air

E♭
Gm
E♭
E♭7
'Cause you're sen - sa - tion - al
'Cause you're sen - sa - tion - al
B♭m7
E♭7
A♭m
A♭
C9
A♭m6
Fm7
B♭9
Mak - ing love is quite an art
Mak - ing love is quite an art
mf
B♭7
E♭
B♭7
What you re - quire is the prop - er squire to
What you should meet is a maid - en sweet to
A7
E dim.
C7
Fm7
B♭7
A♭
fire your heart, And if you say that
heat your heart, And if you say that

Fm7 Fm6 B♭7 Fm7 B♭7 Fm7 B♭7 B♭m6 D♭ B♭m
one fine day you'll let me come to call — We'll have a ball
one fine day you'd like to come to call — We'll have a ball
C7 B dim. C7 Fm7
'Cause you're sen - sa - tion - al, sen -
'Cause you're sen - sa - tion - al, sen -
B♭9 B dim. Cm Gm A♭6 D
sa - tion - al That's all, that's all, that's
sa - tion - al That's all, that's all, that's
1. E♭ 2. E♭
all. all.
f
mp
f
sf

Frank Sinatra, Grace Kelly in HIGH SOCIETY (1956)

Mitzi Gaynor, Kay Kendall, Taina Elg in LES GIRLS (1957)

CA, C'EST L'AMOUR

"Les Girls"

Words and Music by
COLE PORTER

Copyright © 1956 (unpub.) & 1957 by Chappell & Co., Inc.

A♭m
Gm
B♭7
E♭
turn, Ça, c'est l'a - mour.
E♭7
A♭m
E♭m
Then dawns a drear - y day, Your dar - ling goes a -
F7
A♭m6
way And all is o - ver, you are sure.
B♭7
E♭
B♭7
But oh, when she re - turns And loves you as be -
mf
p

Fm7
Bb7
fore, You take her in your lone - ly arms and
Eb
Fm
Eb7
Ab
Bb7
want her e - ven more, Ça, c'est l'a -
mf più espressivo
Gm7
C7
Abm
D
Bb7
mour. Ça, c'est l'a -
1. Eb
2. Eb
mour. When mour.
mf
8va
mf
Ped.
*

WOULDN'T IT BE FUN

"Aladdin"

Copyright © 1958 by Cole Porter
Chappell & Co., Inc., owner of publication and allied rights throughout the world

G7
C
G7
C
F7
Would - n't it be fun not to be known as An im -
Would - n't it be fun not to have al - ways Dead - ly
mf
B♭
D7
G7
C
por - tant V. I. P.? Would - n't it be
di - plo - mats for tea? Would - n't it be
cresc.
E7
Am
A7
Dm7
fun to be near - ly a - ny one ex - cept me,
fun to be near - ly a - ny one ex - cept me,
f
To Patter
Final Ending
G7
C
B7
C
Might - y me!
Mixed - up me!
ff
8

Patter (slightly slower)
Em
Am
B
Yes - ter - day I had to en - dure a kite fly - ing match— And
mp
Em
A7
B
rush to an ex - e - cu - tion down - town.
f
Em
Am
B
Then I gave a lunch-eon for some hor - ri - ble hec - tic Huns who pro-
mp
Em
Am6
B
Em
ceed - ed to drink too much and fall down.
f

G Cm D7
Af - ter lunch I went to in - spect a slave la - bor camp_ And
mp
G A7 D D maj. 7 D7
o - pened a new wing in my dun - geon keep.
mf
G G7 Cm Cm6
Then I gave a feast for a lof - ty La - ma from Ti - bet And he
mp
G Em C6 D7 G G9 G
stayed so late I ne - ver got to sleep, So help me Bud - dha!
cresc.
f

SHOW-FILM CHRONOLOGY

A listing of the 58 songs contained in this book, the shows from which they came, and the artists who introduced them